Gifts From The Heart

450 SIMPLE WAYS TO MAKE YOUR FAMILY'S CHRISTMAS MORE MEANINGFUL

Virginia Brucker

We Believe Publications

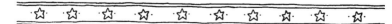

The recipes and ideas for this book were provided by family members, friends, and colleagues. If an error or omission has been made in terms of acknowledgement or permission, the author and publisher warrant that it has been made inadvertently and express regret. We trust that the originating author or publisher will treat its one-time use in this publication as a gift to cancer research. The author and publisher welcome any information enabling them to rectify any reference or credit in subsequent editions.

Canadian Cataloguing in Publication Data

Brucker, Virginia, 1953-
Gifts from the heart

Includes index.
ISBN 0-9686996-0-X

1. Christmas. I. Title.
GT4985.B78 2000   394.2663   C00-910402-X

ATTENTION FUNDRAISERS. Quantity discounts are available on bulk purchases of this book for sales promotions, premiums or fundraising. For information please contact:

WE BELIEVE PUBLICATIONS
Special Sales Department
P.O. Box 47
Nanoose Bay, B.C.
Canada V9P 9J9
Phone or Fax: 250-468-9888

Cover artwork by Caitlin Jewell
Book design by Kari-Lyn Owen, of Klassen Design
Printed and bound in Canada by Transcontinental Printing

This book is dedicated to families everywhere.

A special thank you to Caitlin Jewell, the talented ten year-old who created the art work for the front cover, to Paula Young, who provided the craft project illustrations, and to Kari-Lyn Owen, of Klassen Design, the book's designer. Thanks to all the young artists and writers, and their parents, who graciously granted permission for their work to appear in this book. Another special thanks to my husband, Charlie, and to family members and friends who have been helpful and patient with me over the past two years. I couldn't have managed without you!

Many bookstores, businesses, schools, and organizations are helping raise research funds for the Canadian Cancer Society by selling this book. Your help is greatly appreciated.

I would like to thank all of the volunteers, both young and old, who give their time to the Canadian Cancer Society or to other causes which hold special meaning for them. You enrich our lives.

Thank you, each and every one. May all your Christmases be merry!

Table of Contents

Do all the good you can,
In all the ways you can,
To all the people you can,
In every place you can,
At all the times you can,
As long as ever you can.

~ Shaker Creed

The best parts of a good man's life are his little, nameless
unremembered acts of kindness and love.

~ William Wordsworth

Introduction

For twenty years, I have had a lot of fun working with five to nine year-olds. I hesitate to say I am their teacher, for they have taught me more than I could ever teach them. I am inspired daily by the natural kindness and generosity of children. Kids love to give, and they love to help. All they need is the time, encouragement and appropriate opportunities to reach out to others. One of the ways the children I work with like to help others is by walking or running for Terry Fox. Each September, they talk about parents, grandparents, aunts, uncles and cousins who have had cancer. The run has special significance for us. During the past few years, our small school has lost four parents and our secretary to various forms of the disease.

Like you, I really want families to be able to spend Christmas with the people they love, so the royalties from this book are being donated to cancer research. If you like it, please consider picking up an extra copy or two for gifts —you will be helping a very worthwhile cause!

I hope you find many easy, practical ideas in this book which will help you and your family give your own, unique "gifts from the heart." Wouldn't it be wonderful if we could create more loving Christmases which allow us to reach out to each other and to our communities? Let's begin a tradition of "not so random acts of Christmas kindness," where families, schools, churches, service organizations, and youth groups such as Brownies and Cubs undertake small projects which make our holidays more meaningful.

May you have the best of Christmases, this year, and in all the years to come!

CHAPTER 1

The Gift of Giving

Sam R., age 8

Christmas Acts of Kindness

- give money to the poor
- give love to your family
- be peaceful with your friends
- Send money to the red cross
- Send Food to the Food Bank

by Demitra B,
age 7

"Example is not the main thing in influencing others.
It is the only thing." ~ Albert Schweitzer

Children love to give—it's fun to watch a loved one's face light up when they open a handmade card or gift. Young children enjoy sharing; the challenge is helping them maintain their enthusiasm for giving as they grow older. But if you model generosity at every opportunity when your children are young, they are likely to grow up to be generous, thoughtful people too.

How do you begin? Early in the fall, have a meeting to brainstorm all the possible acts of "Christmas kindness" you can think of. Listen carefully to your children—they'll have lots of good ideas to share. Consider your family's strengths and interests and narrow down the choices. Are you great pet-lovers? You'll find some wonderful ideas in Chapter 12, "An Animal Lover's Christmas." Do your kids miss having older relatives around? You'll find lots of ways to connect with seniors in Chapter 15, "Remembering Seniors at Christmas."

It's easy to become overwhelmed during the holidays. Try choosing just one project to get you started. If you have very young children, making gifts for grandparents is a great way to encourage giving. Chapters 18, 19 and 20 have lots of kid-tested projects that are fun to do. If your children are older, there are many projects they can undertake with very little help. Whenever possible, let your children choose the project and then provide the support, encouragement and materials necessary for their success.

As well as considering the amount of time you can find, think about your family's finances. What kind of project best matches your wallet? You may have time to share, or you may find it easier to give money. Ideally, we'd like to give both, but it's one of the facts of life that we seldom have time *and* money together. You can make money gifts more meaningful for your children by having them count the coins or bills, and by involving them in the shopping, wrapping, or mailing of your donation.

With your help, even very young children can make meaningful contributions. Here are some suggestions to get your family started:

- Collect your change all year long in a family "giving box." Decorate a jar or box early in January and save as much as you can for next Christmas's special projects.

- Sign up for savings bond deductions through your payroll at work. Set aside some of your savings for your own shopping and use part to make a donation to a special cause.

- Give your children a small allowance and provide the following guidelines: one third is for spending, one third is for saving and one third is for sharing. Let your children decide how to donate their sharing portion. Help your children save part of their allowance to purchase or make gifts for their brothers or sisters and other family members. It's easier for very young children to understand the concept of giving to the family first and then to extend it to a charity or the community.

- Help your children go through the toys collected from

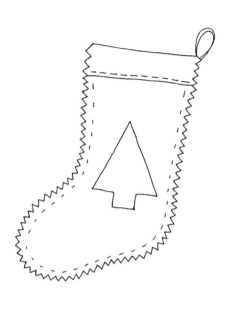

fast food restaurants. Check to make sure they are in good shape. Make some simple felt stockings or decorate lunch bags with Christmas drawings or stickers. Add some well-wrapped Christmas candy and drop the bags off at a soup kitchen. The kids who eat lunch there will enjoy receiving a special Christmas goodie bag.

- Host a "giving party" where children or teens get together and make cookies, small gifts, ornaments or cards to give away.

- Make up a Christmas care package for someone at college or for a neighborhood family who has moved away. Include some drawings and letters, Christmas music, decorations, and of course, a tin of their favorite Christmas treats.

- Have a baby shower at your church, daycare or school. Decorate a big box or borrow a cradle for the manger. Add a doll to represent Jesus. Encourage families to bring items a baby needs such as warm clothing, crib sheets, formula, diapers and sleepers. Donate them to a transition house, shelter or young mothers' group.

- Slip a gift certificate for a food store in a Christmas card. Give it anonymously to a friend, family at school, co-worker or neighbor who needs a little help this year.

- Early in November, help your children look through their toy box and closets for items to donate to your local thrift store or family shelter. Make sure the toys and clothing are in good shape; wash and mend anything that needs sprucing up.

- Decorate a large cardboard box with Christmas wrap early in the fall. Every time you grocery shop, help your child pick out a non-perishable food item to put in the box. Try to include some treats as well as staples; pancake mix, syrup, hot chocolate and marshmallows would make someone's Christmas breakfast special. Drop it off at your local food bank together.

Giving at Work

Make helping others an annual tradition at your workplace. Instead of exchanging gifts with co-workers at your office this year, pick a charity to help. If each person donates a few dollars, it will add up to a sizable donation.

We Are Having A Teddy Bear Toy Drive !

By Tygra S., 10

We can save coats.

By Jessica. O.
Age 8

You could also:

• Start a teddy bear drive. Police officers and hospitals often give bears to children who have been traumatized. Use the bears to decorate your office or school entrance until it's time for them to go to their new homes. If you put up a notice explaining your project, people who visit your office or business may want to contribute a bear. Because kids love stuffed toys, this is also a great project for a school or preschool.

• Collect small items like toiletries and candy for a shelter or hospital. On your lunch hour, have a "work bee" where you all work together to fill small baskets, bags or stockings. You can make simple felt stockings with pinking shears and some glitter glue! Serve hot chocolate and cookies and play Christmas music softly while you work.

• Organize a warm coat collection. Do any necessary mending and wash or dry-clean the coats. You may find a local dry cleaner will volunteer to do them for free. (If so, make a large poster thanking the cleaner for his/her help to be displayed in their window. Perhaps their customers will bring in more coats!) Publicize your coat drive in the local newspaper. When the coats are ready to distribute, tuck some warm mittens or gloves and a Christmas treat in each pocket, and donate your collection to a local shelter, The Salvation Army, a preschool or needy school.

CHAPTER 2

Volunteering as a Family

Santa is so busy, he needs
Kids to be elues too!

Kristen D., 7

If you give money, spend yourself with it.
~ Henry David Thoreau

Children make great volunteers—they are full of enthusiasm, energy, and optimism. There are many good reasons why kids *should* volunteer. Studies show that people who help others are healthier and happier. When children volunteer, their self-esteem is enhanced as they learn new skills and make new friends. They see themselves as kind people capable of making a difference, and they learn to live more hopefully. They develop a stronger, richer sense of self and often have greater empathy and compassion; volunteer activities help build character and teach social responsibility.

Helping others is particularly important for teens. Those who do volunteer show less "at risk" behavior—they are more likely to stay in school, stay out of trouble, and stay off drugs. They may develop a better appreciation of their own family too. Volunteering also helps offset some of the materialism of our culture. It helps children of all ages see that who you *are* is more important than what you *have*. But the most important reason for volunteering is because it's the right thing to do.

The key to getting your children to volunteer is to find a cause they really identify with, whether it's helping the environment, animals or other kids. You will, of course, want to consider your children's safety and supervision very carefully. Children should never go unaccompanied door to door to collect for a cause. You will want to accompany your young children when they volunteer, and even if they are teens, you should go along for the first visit or two.

Your family can:

- Deliver meals at Christmas for Meals on Wheels. Regular volunteers may be out of town during the holidays and extra help may be needed.

- Sort food at a food bank.

- Help serve a Christmas meal on Christmas Day at a shelter or mission.

- Organize a Christmas dance at school or church. Ask the teens attending the dance for a donation or to bring items like toys or food for a local charity.

- Make a pillow, quilt or stockings for a shelter or Ronald McDonald House. This is a great project for a home-ec class, youth group or 4-H club.

- Sports-minded families can help with your local Special Olympics program. Even if you can't make a long-term commitment, you can help with the Christmas party or donate new or gently-used sports equipment.

- Shop for another child and donate the gift to The Salvation Army, a shelter or a transition house. Gifts for older kids and teens are always in short supply. Here's a list of appropriate items provided by a group that works extensively with teens:
    backpacks, blank journals, flashlights, sleeping bags, movie passes, art supplies, gift certificates to a music store, fast food coupons, board games, an inexpensive watch, a walkman, make-up kits, hair care products, baseball caps, earrings, sewing kits, school supplies, gift certificates to a hair salon,

toiletries, flannel shirts, oversized T-shirts, sleepshirts, a prepaid phone card, tube socks, gloves, long johns, and playing cards.

- Donate items your family has outgrown such as a crib, bedding, baby clothes, or baby toys along with some baby food or diapers to a local shelter.

- Organize your teen and some friends to offer a "Mom's Day Out" so parents can have half a day to go shopping. This is a super project for your church's youth group. Help the teens plan a simple program with crafts, snacks, and perhaps a Christmas video. An adult and a good first-aid kit should be on hand in case of an emergency.

- Volunteer at the pet shelter.

- Organize a toy drive for a daycare center or transition house. Contact the center first to see what types of toys are needed.

- Make craft kits with the instructions and materials necessary for a holiday project. Wrap the top and bottom of a shoebox separately to put the items in, and donate the kits to the children's ward of your local hospital.

- Have a pajama party. Instead of wearing pajamas, ask kids to *bring* pajamas to donate to a family shelter.

- Teens can organize a food drive through their school, youth group or sports team. Items such as juices, soups, pasta products, cereals, tinned fruit, canned meat and vegetables, baby food, soap, shampoo, and toothpaste are always needed.

- Make simple stockings or buy small gift bags to fill with items like candy, packages of chips, gum, mittens, toiletry items, socks, or a music tape. Donate the stockings or bags to a shelter or to street kids. This is a great youth group project.

- Bake Christmas treats for a family or an organization that needs your help. Rice Krispie squares can be tied up with long thin pieces of red licorice to look like packages. Cupcakes are easy to dress up with red or green icing and a gummy bear on top.

- Teens can set up a Christmas wrapping station in a local mall to raise money for a charity that has special meaning for them.

- Collect school supplies or books for a family shelter or a school that needs them.

- Make some decorations, placemats or table centers for a shelter or mission that serves Christmas dinner.

- Organize a big buddy tutoring program where teens help "at risk" children with reading.

"Those who bring sunshine to the lives of others cannot keep it from themselves."
~ James Matthew Barrie

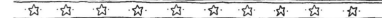

CHAPTER 3

Making Time

Christmas should be a joyous, magical time for children, as well as a time for families to create loving legacies of rich memories. Sadly, many people find the holidays another source of stress in an already hectic life! Often they'll tell you they can't wait until Christmas is over so they can have a rest. It *is* hard to make time in our already crowded schedules for baking, shopping, wrapping, decorating, school concerts and entertaining. How can we possibly organize our own Christmas and undertake some volunteer projects too? We can begin by modifying our expectations. Decide what can be reasonably accomplished and let some of the "have to's" go. Make a conscious decision to *do* less and *enjoy* it more!

Put your energy into creating a more satisfying Christmas that focuses on people rather than on gifts. Hug people and write letters telling friends and family what you love about them. Watch some of those wonderful classic Christmas movies together. Laugh often. Spend your time with family and friends. Set aside one day to help a cause or a friend who really needs your support.

Being organized is one of the best Christmas gifts you can give yourself. Try to finish your shopping and get your cards ready by the end of November. Bake easy-to-freeze treats late in October or buy your baking instead! In December, you'll be able to visit old friends, attend a Christmas performance of the Nutcracker, or take youngsters to a Christmas lunch and movie. If you *do* have to shop in December, visit one of the excellent craft fairs or specialty stores nearby.

- Have a family meeting. Mark off special concerts and parties on the calendar and block in the events your family really loves. Make a list of some of the things you don't enjoy, and wherever possible, cross them off! Brainstorm creative solutions for others. Share the responsibilities.

- Save some of your annual vacation so you can take time off work during December to spend with your children when school is out. If that's not possible, schedule some vacation time in November so that you can get organized. And if *that* won't work, take one day of banked overtime each week.

- Try hard not to get too busy with social commitments that do not involve your family. You can always visit with your co-workers and friends in the long winter months ahead. This time with your children cannot be recaptured later on.

- Make a list of the jobs to be done, and start delegating. Things may not be done exactly as you like them, but you can adjust. Refuse to be a perfectionist.

- If you can't avoid shopping in December, go earlier in the day as well as earlier in the week.

- Pick up Christmas wrap, bags, cards and ribbon on sale after the holidays. Gift bags and tissue make wrapping easier, and the bags can often be recycled for several years.

- Keep a small hardcover book with your list with you at all times. List a couple of choices for each person's gift. Keep the last few years' lists in the same book so you don't give the same present twice.

- Send your spouse out with a detailed list so he/she can

do some of the shopping too.

- Give magazine subscriptions—you don't even have to leave the house to order them!

- Give family gifts rather than individual ones to friends and relatives. You'll save time, wrapping, and money.

- Make a wrapping station by putting all the things you'll need in a tub or box and store it under a table or in a closet. Buy lots of tape.

- Keep all receipts in an envelope in your purse so it's easy to return or exchange items.

- Rather than trudging from store to store, use your phone to shop.

- Looking for a particular item? Let family and friends know what you are looking for so they can call you if they see it; perhaps they can pick it up for you.

- Try theme shopping this year—do most of your shopping in one place. Is there a terrific craft fair you can attend? Can you give several people books from your favorite bookshop? Antique malls, museums, plant nurseries, hardware and office supply stores often have marvelous gifts.

- Don't overspend. You'll be sorry in January; it just creates additional stress and worry. You can never buy enough "stuff" to show people how much you really love them. Find other ways to show how much you care.

- Make sure you don't short change yourself on sleep in

November or December. It never pays off; you'll end up grumpy or sick.

- Get your car serviced in November so that you don't have to worry when travelling over the holidays.

- Trade babysitting with a friend for half a day once a week throughout November. You can get a lot done in three or four hours with no children along. You'll both have more time in December for family outings.

- Plan some easy Christmas craft projects when it's your turn to baby-sit. You'll find lots of good ideas in Chapters 18, 19 and 20. The children will enjoy having handmade gifts to give their family. Wrap them up together so their folks will be surprised.

- Have a weekly family night throughout the fall to make cards, gift tags, ornaments, or baking that can be used in December.

- Use your crockpot to make meals while your family works on Christmas projects. You can find lots of terrific crockpot recipes on the Internet (just do a search under crockpots AND recipes), and there are lots of good cookbooks at the library. Here's a very simple recipe to get you started:

Crockpot Stroganoff

Cut up 2 or 3 lbs. of inexpensive steak into 1-inch pieces, or use pre-cut stewing meat. Put it in the crockpot. Add a package of dried onion soup mix and a can of golden mushroom soup. If you wish, add a can of drained mushrooms and a dash of Worcestershire sauce for a little extra zip. Cook four hours on high or six on low.

Just before serving, add a cup of sour cream and stir gently. Serve with noodles and carrots.

⋅☆⋅ ⋅☆⋅ ⋅☆⋅

- Make double batches of chili and spaghetti early in the fall and freeze some for busy days in December.
- Kids love these meatballs, and you won't believe how simple they are to prepare. Make a batch and tuck them in the freezer.

Barbecued Meatballs

3 lbs. lean ground beef
1-13 oz. can evaporated milk
1 cup oatmeal
1 cup cracker crumbs
2 eggs
1/2 cup finely chopped onion
1/2 tsp. garlic powder
1/2 tsp. pepper
2 tsp. salt

Sauce:
2 cups ketchup
1 cup brown sugar
1/2 tsp. garlic powder
1/4 cup chopped onion (optional)

Meatballs: Combine all ingredients (mixture will be soft)

and shape into walnut-sized balls. Place in single layer on waxed paper lined cookie sheets. Freeze until solid. Store frozen meatballs in freezer bags. (Makes about 80 meatballs, so use half for one meal and save half for another.)

Sauce: Just before baking the frozen meatballs, combine all sauce ingredients and stir until brown sugar is dissolved. Place the frozen meatballs in a 9" by 13" glass baking pan. Pour on the sauce and bake at 350°F for one hour. With rice and green beans, you have a super dinner that kids love! You can also use the same meatballs with pre-made pasta sauce for a quick spaghetti dinner.

·☆·   ·☆·   ·☆·

- No time to do crafts with your children? Many craft stores have excellent workshops for kids. Sign them up so they can have fun while you do some Christmas shopping. Or pick up a couple of good kits with all of the necessary supplies and hire a teenager to help while you wrap gifts or bake.

- Do a thorough house cleaning early in December. Enlist the help of everyone in your family. If you can afford to, hire someone to help with the cleaning; it will help them earn some extra cash for their own Christmas shopping.

- Put away as many knickknacks as you can while cleaning to make room for the Christmas decorations you'll soon be putting out.

- Spread your Christmas decorating throughout December. If you've shopped early, you can spend an hour or two decorating each weekend. Encourage everyone in your family to be responsible for one area. It's their Christmas too!

- Plan some activities like skating, tobogganing, or outdoor walks to collect evergreens for wreaths. Exercise helps minimize stress. Your children will enjoy the time with you, and will be better behaved if they are using up some of that extra energy.

- Participate in a baking exchange. The amount of time spent baking is reduced enormously, and you get to spend an afternoon or evening with your friends. If you're planning to get together in late November or early December, ask everyone to make items that freeze well.

An exchange works well with eleven participants, who each bring twelve dozen of their favorite Christmas treat. Each person should also bring along some tins or plastic storage containers to take their baking home in. Use half of the extra dozen treats each person brought to serve with coffee or tea. Give the other half to someone you know who is unable to bake this year. Wrap a big box with Christmas wrap and put a large bow on the outside, fill the box with your treats and drop it off around the 21st of December!

For your contribution to the baking exchange try these easy, delectable squares:

Raspberry Almond Bars

1 3/4 cups oats
1 cup flour
1 cup brown sugar
1 tsp. baking powder
1/4 tsp. salt
3/4 cup melted butter
3/4 cup raspberry jam
1/2 cup flaked almonds

Combine oats, flour, sugar, baking powder and salt. Stir in melted butter. Mix together until crumbly. Press two-thirds of the crumb mixture into a greased 9" x 9" pan. Spread with jam. Sprinkle remaining crumb mixture on top and top with almonds. Bake at 375ºF for 25 to 30 minutes.

☆   ☆   ☆

• Have potluck dinners when entertaining in December. Your guests will be glad to bring their best company dish. For your contribution, serve this delicious seafood pie—it's incredibly easy and sure to please.

Impossible Seafood Pie

1 cup salmon
1 cup grated sharp cheese
4 oz. package cream cheese
1/4 c. thinly sliced green onion
2 cups milk
1 cup Bisquick

4 eggs
3/4 tsp. salt
dash of nutmeg

Combine the salmon, cheese, cream cheese and green onion in a greased 10" glass pie plate. Blend remaining ingredients on high speed in blender for 15 seconds. Pour over salmon mixture. Add a bit more grated cheese on top. Bake for 35 minutes at 375°F. Let stand 5 minutes before cutting. You can use two small cans of salmon, drained well, or leftover salmon if you have some. Serve with a crisp green salad.

·☆·   ·☆·   ·☆·

Company coming and no time to cook? Try this incredibly easy dish—it's a great way to use up leftovers!

Oven Fried Rice

2 cups uncooked rice (not instant)
3 1/2 cups water
1/2 cup soy sauce
1/2 cup vegetable oil
1 envelope dried onion soup mix (not mixed)
1 chopped onion
1 can mushroom pieces (drained)
1 green pepper, finely chopped
1 stalk of celery, chopped
3 cups of leftover meat—ham, turkey or chicken work well

Mix all ingredients together and cook covered in a large casserole at 350°F for an hour and a half. Now wasn't that simple?

·☆· ·☆· ·☆·

- Have a coffee and dessert buffet where everyone brings a dessert and you provide the coffee, tea and Christmas music. If you need a very quick dessert, you can have this pie in the oven in less than 10 minutes. Use a pre-made frozen pie shell—no one will know!

Raisin Pecan Pie

1 cup sugar
2 beaten eggs
6 tbsp. melted butter
1/4 cup milk
1 cup raisins
1/2 cup chopped pecans

Mix together and bake in an unbaked 8" pie shell at 350°F for 45 minutes. Garnish with real whipped cream or serve with ice cream.

·☆· ·☆· ·☆·

Another very simple to prepare dessert is this pumpkin square recipe. You don't have to fuss with a crust, and it serves 16-20 people easily.

Auntie Elvira's I'll Never Make Pumpkin Pie Again Squares

1-28 oz. can pumpkin
1-13 oz. can evaporated milk
3 eggs
1 cup white sugar
1/4 tsp. salt
2 tsp. pumpkin pie spice (or 1/4 tsp. ginger, 1/4 tsp. nutmeg, 1 tsp. cinnamon and 1/8 tsp. cloves)
1 Duncan Hines yellow cake mix
1 cup melted butter
1 cup chopped pecans or walnuts

Mix the pumpkin, eggs, evaporated milk and spices together and beat well. Pour into an ungreased 9" x 13" pan. Cover with dry cake mix. Drizzle melted butter over the top until completely covered—you may have to use a little more butter. Sprinkle with chopped nuts. Bake at 350°F for 50 minutes, until a knife inserted in the center comes out clean. Chill, and serve with whipped cream.

☆   ☆   ☆

Looking for a quick gift for a teacher, the mailman, or a co-worker? You can't go wrong with this lemon loaf. Many years ago, a dear family friend brought some every couple of weeks to my grandmother who was housebound. Mary's visits were as much appreciated as her delectable treat. Twenty years later I found the recipe and was surprised to see how simple it is. I love it because it only takes a few minutes to prepare, and it makes one delicious loaf to keep and one to give away.

Mary's Luscious Lemon Loaf

1 Duncan Hines lemon cake mix
1 small package lemon Jello
3/4 cup oil
4 eggs

Dissolve Jello in 1 cup of boiling water and let it cool. Blend the cake mix and oil together. Beat in the eggs, one at a time, mixing thoroughly with the electric beater after each addition. Add Jello and mix well again. Pour into two greased and floured loaf pans. Bake at 350°F for 35 to 40 minutes.

While the loaves are still warm, make a glaze with 1/4 cup of lemon juice and 1/2 cup icing sugar or granulated sugar. Poke holes in the loaves with a skewer and pour glaze over the top. Allow to cool in the pan and then wrap well in saran wrap. Serve the next day. Freezes or keeps in the fridge beautifully.

☆   ☆   ☆

- No time to bake? Pick up a batch of your favorite frozen cookie dough like chocolate chip or oatmeal raisin. Add some red and green M & M's. Enjoy the smell of cookies baking in the oven.

CHAPTER 4

The Gift of Gratitude

I'm thankful for: my Swing, me, Carter, mom, Dad, Out Side, my house, Fuzzy My Bear, Food, Friends

by Laura age 6

Things I'm thankful for:

1. my mom
2. my dad
3. my sister Laura
4. Gran
5. Nana
6. Nature
7. my life
8. enough money to support our family
9. our wonderful food
10. a great school

By Carter, age 8

"A thankful heart is not only the greatest virtue,
but the parent of all other virtues." ~ Cicero

Christmas is an ideal time to reflect on the many bless-
ings in our lives and to be grateful for the gifts our hearts
receive each day—children, love, good health, friendship, a
home, good food, books, and pets. Unfortunately, sometimes the real spirit of Christmas gets lost. When we create
a holiday that acknowledges we have much to be thankful
for, we encourage children to lead richer, happier lives.

One of the most important ways we can encourage grat-
itude is to model it ourselves at every opportunity. Make
sure your children know you are grateful for them! Let them
know they are really your greatest blessing. Tell them so
often. When you notice your children being generous or
expressing their appreciation, acknowledge their actions.
That's how they learn what you value, and generous or
appreciative behavior is more likely to become common-
place.

- Make a commitment to spend more time with your family in December.

- Many of the best things about Christmas are free. Spend
  lots of time outdoors. Make angels in the snow while
  you look at the stars together. Be thankful for stars and
  wildlife and trees.

- Help your children write to Santa on Christmas Eve
  thanking him for last year's gift. Leave their notes out
  along with his milk and cookies.

Dear Santa
Thank you for the beads. I really
enjoyed them. Thank you for
telling me about Rudolf.
I had a good time with my
family. I love you.
See you. Next year.
your friend,
BRaiden

- Show your children that little pleasures such as sipping hot chocolate while reading a good story together are to be savored. They will learn to appreciate everyday joys.

- Keep a record in December of how much time you spend with your family and how much time you spend shopping. Is there an imbalance here? What does that tell you?

- Read Antoine De Saint-Exupery's terrific book, *The Little Prince*, together. It has a timeless message of love to share.

- Throughout the year, go around the dinner table occasionally and ask each person to mention something they are grateful for that day. Try to eat together most evenings.

- Speak positively of your friends and family in front of your children. They are more likely to become kind, appreciative people if you do.

- Give your children a small notebook in their stockings to use as a journal to record the things they are grateful for!

- Include a box of thank you cards in your children's stockings. Make it a tradition that Christmas presents can't be used until thank you notes have been written, or set aside part of New Year's Day each year to send notes to friends and relatives.

- If your children are too young to write, you can either write their thank you notes for them or help them phone the gift giver.

- If possible, send a photograph of your children opening or enjoying their gifts along with their thank you note.

- Have your children practice opening imaginary gifts and rehearsing what they will say. Discuss how to acknowledge a gift gracefully even if it is something they already have or don't really want. E.g. "Thank you for the crocheted boxers, Aunt Martha—purple is my favorite color." You can make a game out it, but it will encourage polite and thoughtful responses.

- *Insist* upon acknowledgment of gifts—you are helping your children become the kind of people others will like and enjoy being around.

- Make a special Christmas card for each person in your family to open Christmas morning. Thank them for the special things they do throughout the year.

- Help your children gather the materials needed to make a card for someone important in their lives. Their teacher, bus driver, principal, neighborhood or school librarian, music teacher, sports coach or Cub or Brownie leader don't need a gift, but they will appreciate being remembered at Christmas.

- If you are thinking of a gift, a small gift bag with a few cookies in it is always welcome. This super easy fudge also makes a delicious present. While teens can make it themselves, younger children will need your help.

Super Simple Chocolate Fudge

3 cups semi-sweet chocolate chips
1 can sweetened condensed milk
1 and 1/2 tsp. vanilla
1/2 cup chopped nuts
pinch of salt

Mix condensed milk and chocolate chips in a microwave safe bowl. Microwave on medium-high for one minute. Stir and microwave again for another minute. Stir until blended. Add vanilla, nuts and salt. Stir gently again just until mixed. Turn into a wax paper lined 8" by 8" pan and refrigerate until firm. Cut in squares and keep in the fridge in an airtight container. For individual treats for your child's classmates or friends wrap each piece in saran wrap and then tie them up with curly ribbon to look like tiny Christmas packages. Makes 1 3/4 pounds. (Freezes well.)

☆ ☆ ☆

- If you really feel you need to give your child's teacher a gift, consider giving something which all the children in the class can enjoy, such as a children's tape or CD, a good book for the classroom library, some special stickers or felts, some glitter glue or a package of special computer paper.

- Draw a tree on green poster board and cut out simple paper ornaments. On each ornament, ask your children to draw something or someone they are thankful for. Photographs could also be used. You may also use a small tree or a twiggy branch.

- Encourage your children to make a special point of letting their grandparents know they are loved and appreciated. Give hugs, phone often, make cards!

- Acknowledge the contributions that firemen, policemen, and hospital staff make to our lives. Bake or buy some cookies or muffins. Drop them off with a card that says, "Merry Christmas. Thanks for keeping us safe."

- Bake a simple cake and decorate it with white icing. Help each family member light a candle as he/she makes a wish for the family or for someone or something special.

- Create a sharing tree. Use a tiny tree or a large twiggy branch anchored in a small bucket with sand. Decorate it with handmade ornaments, cookies, cards or paper hearts that your children have written a thoughtful message on. Your children can give each guest something from the "sharing tree" along with a simple, "Thanks for coming to be part of my Christmas."

- Be sure to show your appreciation to store clerks at Christmas. Children need to see their moms or dads model courtesy—that's how they learn good manners.

- Model contentment yourself. If you are always talking about what you wish you had or want to buy, your children will copy your attitude.

"Think contentment the greatest wealth."
~ George Shelley

CHAPTER 5

Fighting the Gimmies

Bailey W, age 6

Don't ask Santa for too many toys.
He can't fit it all in his sleigh.

Where there is too much, something is missing.
~ Anonymous

Christmas is often spoiled by the dreaded "gimmies." You may not be able to get rid of them, but you can reduce them by planning for some unhurried times together and by creating simple family traditions that focus on fun. Here are some tips:

- Reduce the amount of TV your child watches, particularly in November and December.

- Mute the sound during toy commercials.

- Discuss the unrealistic claims made by commercials.

- Let your children buy their toys with part of their allowance. Kids become smart shoppers fast if they are spending their own money.

- Reduce your own debts. Show your children that it is important to be prudent with money. Teach them how to save for that proverbial "rainy day." Learning to manage money well is a terrific gift to give your children.

- Replace television watching with activities like making cards and gifts, reading Christmas stories and baking.

- If your kids really miss TV, rent Christmas videos instead—they don't have commercials, and many emphasize the spirit of sharing and giving.

- One of the biggest reasons parents give too many gifts

is because they feel guilty for working. Try to give the gift of your time—your child won't feel he or she needs to be filled up by getting lots of "stuff."

- If your family is used to lots of presents, you may want to begin reducing the number of gifts gradually. Cut back a little each year. Give some coupons in your children's stockings that promise to take them skating or swimming, to the library or out for a picnic lunch. Make sure you honor your promises.

Gifts That Don't Cost Money

- a book
- a painted rock
- a card
- love
- a smile
- a hug
- a picture
- best manners
- respect
- a kiss

by Tanis M., age 7

- Ask your child to make a list of gifts that don't cost any money, such as a drawing, giving or receiving a hug, getting to ride in the front seat for a whole day or picking the menu for dinner. They should include things they would like to give as well as to receive. Make some of these wishes into coupons to give to each other.

- During the last week of November, make an advent paper chain. Cut 1" by 9" strips of colored construction paper. Number them in order from 1 to 24. On each strip, write down something you will do on the corresponding date in December. For example—attend the Christmas concert, go to Aunt Sheila's, watch *The Grinch*, go shopping for a toy for The Salvation Army's Angel Tree, or bake cookies. Your children can help you generate ideas for the activities. Put the strips in numerical order and build the chain by gluing December 1st's strip into a loop, then sliding the one for December 2nd through and forming the second link, until you've built a chain with twenty-four links. Hang up with the link with the number 1 at the bottom. Make a star to mark the top. Remove one link each day and enjoy the activity described. Count the remaining links to see how many days are left until Christmas. Kids love this project!

- Keep a kindness calendar. Provide your children with a large blank calendar for December where they can record their good deeds. Leave it out on Christmas Eve for Santa to see. Santa can write a note of encouragement back.

- Assign everyone in your family another family member's name. Throughout December, they are that person's "secret elf." Their mission is to perform "random acts of kindness" without being caught. On Christmas morning,

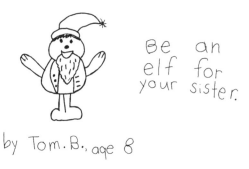

Be an elf for your sister.

by Tom. B., age 8

announce who each "elf" helped.

- Choose a family charity or service project each December. Your children will realize there is more to Christmas than presents for themselves.

- Encourage your children to draw up a list of people they want to give homemade gifts or cards to. It will encourage them to see Christmas as a time for giving as well as for receiving.

- Set reasonable limits for expectations for gifts. If Santa brings everything on your child's list, he won't have room for other kids' presents. And if you *are* giving your child an expensive gift, make that one be from Mom and Dad. It's hard for children to understand why Santa brought their best friend a computer while they got a hockey stick.

- When your children ask for something, acknowledge their wish. "Wouldn't that be nice? Let's add it to your list." Closer to Christmas, ask them to highlight the three items they really want.

- Help pre-schoolers make a short, simple list for Santa. Cut out a construction paper stocking and ask them to draw a picture or cut pictures from a catalog of one big gift and a couple of inexpensive ones that they would like. Label their pictures and mail their list to Santa.

- Your church or school may want to adopt a foster child in another country. It's quite an expensive undertaking for an individual family, but is affordable for a larger group. Study the adopted child's country and share his/her letters and pictures on a bulletin board. It will help children realize that most of us have more than enough and that we should share what we have.

- Encourage well-meaning relatives to consider giving family gifts rather than lots of individual presents. A family pass to the aquarium, planetarium, or a museum, tickets to a Christmas play or concert, a family swimming or skating pass, a magazine subscription the whole family can enjoy, a Christmas video or CD, a board game, a variety of craft supplies and a really good "how to" craft book are all good choices.

- Spread out the excitement of gift opening. Allow your children to open presents when relatives bring them— they will enjoy seeing your children's pleasure. Save some gifts and let your kids open one each day over the twelve days of Christmas. Each gift will feel special.

- Make the opening of gifts last longer Christmas morning. Ask the oldest or youngest person to hand out the presents. Open them one at a time and then pass each one around for everyone to admire.

- Organize the gifts under the tree by the *giver's* name. Each person passes out the presents they are giving and says something thoughtful to the recipient.

- Write gift tags that give clues about the recipient or the gift inside. Each clue must be read and guesses made before the gift is opened.

- Have a Christmas treasure hunt where gifts are hidden and written clues are left all over the house.

- If a gift is too big to fit under the tree, hide it in a closet or the garage. Tie a piece of wool to the end of the present and loop it throughout the house. Fasten the end of the wool to a gift tag and place the tag under the tree. The recipient follows the string to discover the gift. If you are giving just one large gift to each person, it will "stretch out" the fun!

- Introduce a new tradition—each family member must receive at least one homemade present.

- Involve children in making their own gifts or in shopping for others. Too often we pick up something for them to give to Grandma—the kids miss all the fun.

- Read Christmas stories that emphasize the joy of giving at Christmas. *Franklin's Gift* or *Arthur's Christmas* are great for younger children, and O. Henry's classic, *The Gift of the Magi*, is perfect for older ones.

- Young children need to practice actually *giving* a gift. Two or three year-olds may not be able to print their name on the tag, but they can put the gift in someone's hands and give them a hug.

- Think of a silly rule for this year's gifts, such as all presents must start with the same letter as the recipient's name or must cost less than an arbitrary amount such as $3.94. The focus will be on fun rather than on the price of the gift.

- Give gifts that develop your children's interests and abilities. An inexpensive craft kit can keep them happily engaged for a long time.

- Give the gift of music. Research shows that learning an instrument at an early age plays a powerful role in brain development. And even more important, it is good for the soul! If you can possibly afford it, give your child music lessons.

- Cut back on gifts and put the money in educational funds for your children instead. Small amounts add up over time. Having the opportunity to pursue a career which they love is a superb gift.

Thank you
Santa.

By Perry D; 6

CHAPTER 6

Giving the Gift of Imagination

Lego is a great gift!

By kody M. , Age 10

Using Your Imagination

I think that a great gift that would encourage kids to use their imaginations would be a what-not box. This is a box filled with almost anything crafty like: glue guns, pom-poms, pipe cleaners, glue sticks, felts, crayons, pencil crayons, scrap material, string, tape, glitter or glitter glue, paint, paint brushes, ribbon, popsicle sticks, cardboard, scissors, felt, fun foam, wool, lace, straws, wiggily eyes, paper twist, & modge podge. If I were you this is what I would put in a what-not box.

Becky D., age 10

"Imagination is more important than knowledge."
~ Albert Einstein

One of the reasons children have "the gimmies" is because many toys do not really meet their creative needs. Although there are well-designed educational toys on the market today, they are often overlooked in favor of the ones heavily advertised on television. If a well-meaning relative asks what your children would like for Christmas, gently encourage them to look for toys that allow children to be children, rather than mini-consumers of the latest fads.

If you are a baby boomer, think back to your childhood in the fifties or sixties. We didn't have a lot of toys, but the ones we did have were well used—a little red wagon, Lincoln logs, Mechano or Tinkertoy sets, and old clothes worn for dressing up kept us busy. We'd turn over chairs and throw a sheet over the top to make a cave or play house. We made puppets from socks and a puppet theater from a cardboard box. Board games kept us occupied on rainy days and sharpened our math skills. When Christmas shopping this year, try visiting a teacher's store or one of those wonderful shops that specialize in quality science and math toys. You'll find all sorts of fun, durable gifts.

If someone asks you what your child might like for Christmas or if you are shopping for grandchildren or nieces and nephews, here are some suggestions designed to keep children actively engaged and to promote the gift of imagination.

1 to 3 Year-olds

- simple board books
- stacking or nesting toys
- dolls (not too small)
- bath toys
- balls (not too small)
- push and pull toys
- playground toys made of durable plastic
- connecting toys with large beads or links
- mowers or gardening toys
- a paint apron, tip-proof paint pots and large paint brushes
- a sturdy easel
- a well-made wooden rocker
- a simple, sturdy wood or plastic wagon
- smooth wooden blocks
- a beginner's tricycle
- large cars, trucks, trains or wheelbarrows
- a toy telephone
- dress-up clothes

4 to 6 Year-olds

- Lego
- books, puzzles, and plastic models featuring dinosaurs
- a bug house and a book about bugs
- a good magnifying glass
- a scale with two pan balances
- a kaleidoscope
- puppets
- a puppet theater
- a collection of plastic animals and a snap-top storage container to keep them in
- good quality CD's or tapes for children

- an inexpensive (or recycled) tape recorder and some blank tapes
- jewelry-making kits with easy-to-construct projects
- dress-up clothes and a suitcase (often found at thrift stores)
- art supplies
- a child-sized oven
- a plastic bin with a lid and some plastic bottles and a funnel to use as an indoor sand box for rainy days— include a bag of rice, which pours as well as sand, but isn't as messy
- a kid-sized picnic bench set (easy for a relative to build)
- homemade or purchased play dough

Holiday Play Dough

This is a great gift for children. Put the play dough in a clear plastic bag and tie it up with curly ribbon. Add some cookie cutters and a child-sized rolling pin from the dollar store. Tuck it all in a gift bag for a present that will provide hours of fun.

Ingredients:
1 cup flour
1/2 cup salt
2 tsp. cream of tartar
2 tbsp. cooking oil
1 cup of water
food coloring

Mix dry ingredients together in a large bowl. Add oil and water and food coloring next. Place the mixture in a very large pot and cook over medium heat until it gradually forms a ball. Remove the dough from the heat and let it cool. Knead well, then refrigerate in a covered container. After a few hours, knead it again until it is really pliable. Store the dough in a recycled margarine tub in the fridge when not being used.

<u>6 to 8 Year-olds</u>

- a bubble making kit that makes those huge bubbles kids love
- a wooden shelf to keep special treasures on
- a small set of matchbox cars and a carrying case
- a tee ball stand with bat and ball
- a globe
- more dinosaur stuff
- a plastic bead ornament kit
- spool knitting supplies
- a special pillow or a bean bag chair
- a beginner's crochet kit

Kids love getting dinosaurs.

Kalyn, 7

- a plaster casting kit to make fossils
- art kits, a big set of crayons or washable felts
- a cash register with play money
- a modeling clay kit
- a dried flower kit
- nature books about butterflies, insects, rocks, sea life, the rainforest and other animals
- an inexpensive watch
- a coin set for the current calendar year

The best present I ever got was my iguana. Thanks Dad.

by Tyson S., 8 years old

8 to 12 Year-olds

Many of the items above are suitable for 8 to 12 year-olds too. Look at the recommended ages on the product carefully. This age group would also enjoy:

- a friendship bracelet kit
- a microscope
- a calligraphy kit

- a plastic air mattress, flippers, snorkel or a mask
- a starter aquarium kit
- a good quality basketball or soccer ball
- a basketball hoop
- supplies to decorate hair barrettes
- a sewing box with scissors, needles, pins, a measuring tape, thread and some felt squares
- instructions and materials to make simple quilted projects like potholders, a doll blanket, or a wall hanging
- a birdhouse or bird feeder kit with precut wood parts
- a t-shirt and some fabric paints to decorate it with
- a hockey stick and puck or ball for road hockey
- a pair of walkie talkies
- a hockey net
- a sleeping bag for sleep-overs
- inexpensive binoculars
- a magic kit
- a silver locket, bracelet or ring

Teens

Teens are incredibly hard to buy for. It is almost impossible for an aunt, an uncle or a grandparent to choose anything a teen would want to wear, read, or listen to. Clothing is generally rejected just because you picked it; this age group wants to assert their growing independence by choosing their own. Rather than giving a gift that may go unused, try:

- a gift certificate to a favorite music, clothing or book store
- a gift certificate for a course at the local community center or college

- a coupon which promises a contribution to a driver's education program for teens
- a gift certificate for a couple of hours of computer instruction at your local college or one of the smaller computer stores where staff have the time to share their expertise
- a handmade certificate which indicates you have made a donation to the teen's favorite cause, like the S.P.C.A. or Save the Whales
- a savings bond for college
- a cookbook geared for teens
- a sports bag or backpack
- an inexpensive camera
- a tent or sleeping bag
- camping equipment
- a radio with a snooze alarm
- a swim or fitness pass for a month
- a magazine subscription

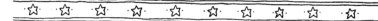

CHAPTER 7

The Gift of Tradition

Dear Santa,

I will leave you peanut butter cookies again next year at Christmas. Thank you for all the wonderful gifts.

your friend,
Lauren B., age 8

"The way you celebrate Christmas can be a gift in itself, handing on traditions that will give your child a feeling of continuity, comfort and joy in all the Christmases to come." ~ Mr. Rogers

Take a few moments to reflect on your Christmases as a child. Did you always put your tree up in front of the picture window in the living room? Did the youngest child put the star on the top of the tree? Perhaps your mother always served a particular meal on Christmas Eve. Did you open one gift before going to bed on December 24th? Simple customs repeated over time become much loved traditions.

While they need not be expensive or time-consuming, traditions *are* important. Research shows that families with them are stronger and more resilient. Children especially look forward to the comfort and security they provide. In good times, traditions say, "Our family is important, we care about you, and we love you." In times of sorrow, they give us comfort. Creating a few simple traditions together is a very meaningful gift to give your children.

When planning new traditions, try and choose some that include family members of all ages—cousins, grandparents, aunts and uncles give children a sense of where they belong in the whole family. If you have a very small family, adopt some elderly neighbors or include old friends. Children need lots of people to love them!

I hope you will find two or three ideas in this chapter which will make your holiday more memorable.

- Just after dark each Christmas Eve, look for Santa in the sky. Can you spot a red light? Is it Rudolph's nose?

- Make a wish for the world on the first star you see each Christmas Eve.

- Leave a small scrap of torn red velvet in the family or living room near the fireplace, or the front door if you don't have a chimney. Tell your children this is the patch that was torn from Santa's pants when he went back up the chimney or out the door.

- Sprinkle some glitter around the fireplace or doorknob after your children have gone to bed on Christmas Eve. The next morning, tell your children this is the magic dust Santa has to use to make himself fit in small places.

- Serve hot chocolate with a candy cane, warm apple juice with a sprinkling of cinnamon, or eggnog. Give special mugs as stocking stuffers.

- Pick a small item to put in stockings every year. It doesn't really matter what you choose—it could be funny socks or underwear. One friend told me her husband's family always put a potato in each person's sock! Her husband didn't know why—his dad always did it, so he does it too.

- If you are having a family gift exchange, you'll enjoy this game. Each family member brings a gift that costs less than $5.00. It should be suitable for any member of the family. One person reads *The Night Before Christmas* aloud. Every time he or she reads the word "the," everyone passes his or her gift to the person on the right. At the end of the story, each person opens the last gift they were passed.

- Create a new ornament together each year.

- Give new pajamas to your children and allow them to open them on Christmas Eve. Snuggly flannel will feel wonderful all through January and February, and your Christmas morning pictures will look great. To make getting the kids to bed early easier, attach a note from Santa saying that he wants the children to go right to bed after putting the pajamas on so that he can visit.

- Put on a play each December with your children. It could be the story of the first Christmas or you can write your own. If a play sounds too complicated, ask your children to sing a familiar song or recite a Christmas poem. Add the new performances to the videotape from past years. Send copies to grandparents who can't attend.

- When your children are a little older, write a family poem or song each Christmas. Use the tune from a song everyone knows, like Jingle Bells. Keep a copy for your scrapbook or put it on a tape.

- Start a Christmas collection. It doesn't have to be expensive. You might save all the cards with snowmen or Santas to put out each year, or you might collect a particular type of ornament or decoration. Don't forget to write the date on each one.

- Hang up some mistletoe. Give family members a hug or a kiss every time you catch them under it.

- Visit Santa together on the same day each year.

- Pick the same day each year to go for a drive to see the lights. Serve your family's favorite supper first, then hop in the car. Take along your favorite Christmas tapes or CD's. Invite someone along who might not see the lights otherwise.

- Buy one new cookie cutter every December to add to your collection.

- Put a Christmas breakfast in your children's stockings. Small juice boxes, granola bars, a muffin or cinnamon bun, and a Christmas orange work well.

- Invite friends to a wreath or cookie-making session each year.

Every year we get invited to a wreath making party. I like to make lots of wreaths for lots of people. I gave two of my wreaths to my Nana and her friend.

Annie S., Age 10

- Make a fruit salad together on Christmas Eve. Ask each family member to help prepare a fruit. Mix it all up and serve it with cinnamon rolls or banana bread for an easy breakfast Christmas morning.

- When you put away your Christmas decorations each year, fill a baggie with cinnamon sticks and some whole cloves. Poke a tiny hole in the bag to allow the scent to escape. When you open your boxes next year you'll be surrounded by the delicious scent of Christmas.

- Learn some Christmas poems to recite together at the dinner table in December.

- If you no longer have children at home, attend a Christmas concert at a nearby school. It will really give you the Christmas spirit! Call ahead to check the date and time first. Most schools have a dress rehearsal which is usually not as well attended so you are more likely to find a seat. If you are helping put on a concert at your preschool, school or church, invite local seniors to attend your dress rehearsal.

- Make a holiday "fun jar." Write down activities such as "Read a Christmas book together," or "Bake your favorite cookies," on small slips of paper. Put them in the jar and let the family member who has shown the most Christmas spirit choose a slip for that day's activity.

- Feed the birds every Christmas Eve or Christmas afternoon.

- Buy a new board game each December and learn how to play it together.

- Start a Christmas jigsaw puzzle on December 1st. Try to have it completed by Christmas Eve.

"A family may not live under one roof, still it lives in one heart."
~ Anonymous

CHAPTER 8

Oh Christmas Tree

Shane M., age 8

I love gazing at
the Christmas tree and
looking at the dazzling
decorations that all 3 kids
made. I love the flickering lights
that make you smile. I love
sitting in front of the
Christmas tree that shines.
by Kristen L, age 9

"Of all the gifts I have each year (some sparkling bright and glowing), I think the gifts I hold most dear, are the ones so green and growing." ~ *Anonymous*

What would Christmas be without a tree? When you close your eyes, can you still see the trees of your childhood? While they didn't resemble the lush, cultured trees popular now, to a child each one was magical. The sweet smell of a freshly-cut fir is one of the most delightful pleasures of the holiday season. My best friend Sheila has a small tree farm where families can enjoy a glass of hot apple cider or cookies made with honey from her own hives before picking out their tree. What a wonderful outing for families! If you look in the yellow pages of your phone book, you may discover a terrific tree farm near you to visit.

When you buy your tree locally, you have the assurance of knowing it will be fresh and therefore, more fire resistant. Trees purchased from large chain stores are often cut in October or early November, and dry out quickly once inside the house. Remember to take a tape measure and a sturdy rope to tie the tree to your car with. Call ahead for directions and hours of operation. Dress for the weather— warm jackets, boots, mittens and hats will make you all more comfortable. If you don't have a tree farm nearby, consider buying your tree from the Boy Scouts. They really appreciate your support.

Can't decide between a real tree and an artificial one this year? It may help you make up your mind if you consider the following:

- Real Christmas trees are renewable and recyclable. Artificial trees contain plastic and metals that do not break down in landfills. Manufacturing artificial trees requires lots of chemicals which end up in the air or water.

- Real trees can be cut up for mulch and compost.

- For every live tree that is cut down, several seedlings are planted. Millions of trees grown especially for Christmas produce much-needed oxygen while they are growing.

- Real Christmas trees provide employment opportunities for people locally.

- Buying a real tree is environmentally sound because it requires less energy than transporting an artificial one made on the other side of the world.

Some "tree traditions" to consider:

- Shop for your tree at the same tree farm or Boy Scout lot each year.

- Take the whole family tree hunting every year. Include grandparents, your own brothers and sisters and your children's cousins. Take turns having a potluck dinner after the families have selected their trees. No family close by? Then go with your best friends.

- Place the tree in the same spot in your house each year.

- Put up your tree on the same date every December.

- Commemorate your baby's first Christmas by planting a tiny Christmas tree in the yard.

- When it's time to decorate the tree, put on a Christmas CD and get the whole family involved. Assign each person a part of the tree to be responsible for. Mom, Dad or big brother or sister can do the lights. Younger children can decorate the bottom with unbreakable ornaments. Your tree may not look like the ones in glitzy magazines, but the memories of your time spent together will last forever.

- Give your children an ornament each Christmas to represent a special event in their lives from the past year, such as ballet slippers for the new dancer, skates for the skater, or a dog or cat ornament the year a new pet joined your family. You can find hundreds of ornaments at a Christmas specialty store. Craft sales often have very reasonably priced ones. If you enjoy crafts, you can make your own.

- Let the youngest person present put the star or angel on the top while everyone else closes their eyes and makes a wish.

- Sing the same carol in front of the tree after you've turned on the lights for the first time.

- Invite the same relatives or friends to come and have hot chocolate and cookies while you decorate the tree together.

- Make or buy a Christmas tree skirt. If you have a young family, look for one made from washable fabric. A round red or green tablecloth can be turned into a tree

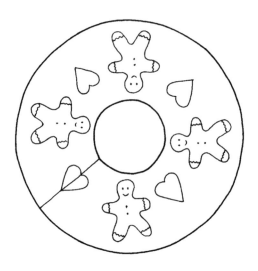

skirt quite easily. Use a small plate to trace a circle in the middle of the tablecloth. Cut out the circle. Fold the tablecloth in quarters and cut along one fold to form the opening. Finish the raw edges by turning them over and zigzagging with matching thread.

You can trace your family members' hands and then outline handprints with a fabric pen or paint. (Print each person's name inside his or her handprint.) You can also stamp gold stars or gingerbread men on and then label each one with a family member's name. Look for a type of compressed sponge called Miracle Sponge at your local craft store. Cut out the shape you want and then soak the sponge in water. Squeeze it out well and then pounce it up and down on a tray of fabric paint. Stamp the sponge on the fabric carefully. Let dry and embellish with fabric paints.

Felt is even easier to work with. Cut a 45" or 60" circle from red, dark green or blue felt. Trace some cookie cutters on various colors of felt and sew or glue the cut out shapes onto the skirt. Add some sequins and fabric glitter glue if you like. For a country-style skirt, use embroidery thread to buttonhole stitch your appliques onto the felt. Embellish each one with some buttons.

- If you can't make a tree skirt, put it on your Christmas list as a possible family gift. Check out craft fairs too.

- Let children have their own tiny Christmas tree in their room to decorate as they wish. Use some shiny gold garland rather than electric lights.

- Santa's elves love to stop by so they can tell him how wonderful your family's tree looks. The morning after you've put up the tree, leave a little note and a small treat or an ornament from the elves!

- Save a piece of your Christmas tree's trunk for next year's Yule log. Burning it is supposed to bring you good luck! You may want to try an old English tradition. Before lighting the log, place one sprig of holly for each family member on top. Each person makes a wish as the Yule log burns.

CHAPTER 9

Making Memories

kids Love snow men and kids all so Love making snow men.   Alex D., 7

Browsing through photographs of the children sitting on Santa's knee or opening gifts under the tree is a wonderful way to recall past holidays spent with the people we love. If you are like many families who grew up during the fifties and sixties, you may not have a lot of photos—cameras, film and developing were expensive in those days. Why not preserve your family's Christmas memories by making a tape or video of your Mom and Dad talking about the Christmases when you were growing up? Include some funny anecdotes as well as favorite stories about family members who are no longer alive.

- If you are a grandparent, one of the best gifts you can give your children when their first baby is born is a camera!

- Have your children's picture taken with Santa each year. Make a special display on the buffet or mantle or put the photos in an album to display on the coffee table during December. If you can afford to, get multiple copies so each of your children may have their own set some day. Collect the photos in special albums; they will make wonderful gifts when your children move out on their own.

- After Christmas, get multiple sets of your family's Christmas pictures. Give each child an album as one of their Christmas gifts. Let them write their own captions under each print. Make sure you record the dates too.

- Take a picture under this year's tree to include in next year's card.

- Keep a loaded camera within easy reach throughout Christmas. The best opportunities come when least expected.

- Store your pictures all year long in one drawer or in a plastic bin with a lid. Over the Christmas holidays, set aside a day to reminisce while you put them in albums.

- Make a video for a family member who can't come home for Christmas this year. Ask each family member to add a special "I love you because..."

- Make an audio or videotape with Grandma and Grandpa. What was their most memorable Christmas like? What did they do on their Christmas vacation once school was out? Was there usually snow? Did they skate or toboggan? What was their most memorable gift? Did they make gifts for their family? What do they remember about their school Christmas concerts? If they grew up in another country, what kind of traditions did their family have?

- Tape your children reading a Christmas story. Add to the tape each year.

- Store your negatives with another family member or in a fireproof box. In the event of a fire, you'll be able to replace your precious photos.

Besides photos, there are lots of other ways to revisit the "spirits of Christmas past":

- Make up a family Christmas trivia game. Each family member interviews another and writes down several questions on one side of a file card and the answers on the other. Very young children will need someone to help write their cards. Mix up the cards, form a couple of teams, and have fun. Save the cards from this year to add to the game next year.

- Make a "Christmas box" from an old trunk, suitcase, or cardboard box. Decorate it simply. After Christmas is over, ask each family member to choose a special card, a piece of clothing, an art project from school or a photo to add to the memory box.

- Do you have a new baby? Start a special Christmas album and invite family members and guests to write in it. Store the album along with their first Christmas outfit; someday it will make a great gift for their first Christmas as a newlywed or new parent.

- Buy or make a baby's first Christmas ornament for each child. Give one as a gift at baby showers. (If you can afford to, buy one for the baby and one for the parents to keep when the children move out.)

- Save your child's first Christmas outfit. Put it on a teddy bear or doll and use it as part of your Christmas decorations.

- Save your children's tiniest mittens or shoes. Add some ribbon and a bell to turn them into tree ornaments.

- Put one of those ornaments which hold a small photograph in your children's stocking each year. Write the date on the back! Display them on your family tree or create a smaller memory tree from a large bare branch.

- Discuss your family's special holiday memories while eating Christmas dinner.

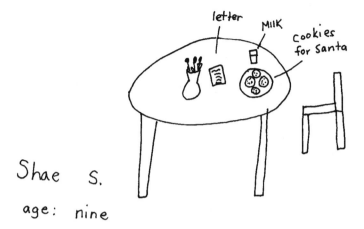

letter

MIlK

cookies
for Santa

Shae S.

age: nine

- Set aside an evening in December to have a quiet date with your spouse. Talk about your Christmas memories as a couple.

- Watch your favorite Christmas movie with your family.

- Pick the same date each year such as the first Sunday in December for your children to write to Santa. Tuck their letters in their boots or slippers for Santa's elves to pick up. Spirit the originals away for a memory book. If you send letters to Santa via the fire in the chimney, make a copy first.

- Keep copies of your annual Christmas card letter, one for each child and one for you. They make a wonderful record of the important events and milestones in your lives. When your children are old enough, encourage them to add their own news to your family's letter.

- Make Christmas pillows or wall hangings from plain muslin squares. Ask your children to draw a picture on the muslin with permanent felts or fabric pens. Sew a bright border cut from Christmas fabric around the square and attach a backing if it's going to be a wall hanging. If you are making pillows, make a pillow slipcover that fits over pillows you already have so you don't have to buy extra forms.

• Give newlyweds a special ornament for their first Christmas. A box of decorations and some mini-lights, a tree skirt or Christmas stockings make great wedding gifts. If you make the stockings yourself, tuck a yard or two of the fabric into the box so the family can make more stockings for future arrivals.

• If a special bride is having her dress made, try and obtain some scraps of the fabric to dress an angel for the top of the newlyweds' tree. You can buy an inexpensive angel and make a new "overskirt" from a small piece of leftover bridal fabric. You could also use the scraps to make an ornament, cuffs on stockings or incorporate them as part of a tree skirt.

• Give newlyweds a collection of your family's favorite Christmas recipes along with a Christmas cookbook.

• Save a piece of your first Christmas tree as newlyweds, as well as from each year a new family member arrives. Drill a hole and make an ornament out of it. You can "modge podge" a photo onto the wood quite easily.

Record the date and event on the back with a permanent felt pen.

- Give some of your special treasures for gifts—a book you have always loved, a beautiful teacup, a family brooch or ring. Encourage the recipient to open the gift with you present so you can enjoy their response.

I love looking at the decorations I made. I think its' good that I make decorations because they give you memories that you could never forget. I think its good that I give the decorations away because then other people can enjoy them too!

By Bryn J., age 9

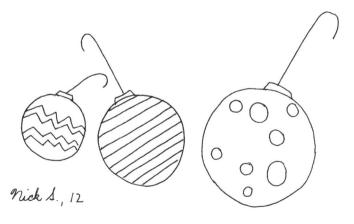

Nick A., 12

- Save some of your children's Christmas artwork from year to year to create a unique display. It makes young artists feel very special. Pick up inexpensive frames at garage sales.

- Write a letter or make a tape for your husband or wife. Tell them why you love and appreciate them. Wrap it up with a big red bow—it will be their best present!

- Write a letter to your parents thanking them for making your holidays special. Describe some of your favorite memories. Thank them for being your parents. Tell them you love them. Keep a copy for your own Christmas memory box.

- If you are upset with a family member, try to make peace with them over the holidays. Send a card or phone. Life is too short to harbor grudges for long.

- Create a time capsule after Christmas to open in ten, twenty or thirty years. Ask your children to add drawings they've made of the family.

CHAPTER 10

Christmas and Divorce

I made a stocking for you.

by Shawna J.
Age 7

"Hard words bruise the heart of a child."
~ Longfellow

Most of us have a vision of Christmas that includes two loving parents and a couple of happy children. We wish it were so. Over half of today's children will experience Christmas as part of a divorced family; many will join blended families with all the complications that combining two sets of children entails. Some will spend Christmas with a parent who is still grieving for the loss of their marriage. Divorce is hard on children, parents and grandparents; there is so much anger, pain and resentment. Many of you may feel anything but "merry" as you adjust to the pressures and financial worries of single parenting. Christmas may feel like an impossible challenge this year. Here are some practical suggestions for coping with the holidays as a divorced parent or as a step-parent. Perhaps they will help you give your children the gift of peace and harmony between the two households.

- Make decisions about "who is going where with whom" long before Christmas holidays actually start. Let your children know what the plans are and why the decisions have been made this way. Involve them in the planning if possible.

- Consider having your children spend Christmas Eve with one parent and Christmas Day with the other. That way both parents can enjoy seeing the children open their gifts.

- Listen carefully to what your children want to do about traditions. Some children will really need the comfort of old family rituals. Others may prefer to create new ones. Have a family meeting in November to discuss their preferences.

- Help your kids buy or make a gift for their mom or dad and their other set of grandparents. Even if it is hard for you to do, it's really important.

- Give your children what may be the best gift of all. Either say positive things about their other parent or say nothing at all.

- Give gifts that encourage your children to stay in touch with you or your ex. Long distance phone cards, stationery, a tape recorder and tapes help kids stay connected.

- Try hard to maintain a cordial relationship with your ex-in-laws. Don't deny relatives access just because you are angry with your former spouse. Kids need lots of people to love them!

- When you take your Christmas film in to get developed, get an extra set of prints. Your kids can make albums for mom/dad and grandparents to give as gifts.

- Don't fall into the "feeling guilty" trap of buying tons of gifts. Spend more time doing things with your children instead, not only at Christmas, but throughout the year.

- Write a special holiday letter to each of your children. Tell them what you love and admire most about them. If you aren't able to give it to them this year, put it away in a special memory box.

- Consider spending Christmas in a new place or with

special friends this year; the first holiday on your own is especially difficult.

- Be sensitive to your children's moods and needs. If both households are trying to fit in lots of activities, there may be too much excitement. Choose calming activities; read together, bake cookies, go for walks, and play board games.

- If you are going to be alone at Christmas, be extra good to yourself. Arrange special visits with friends and family. Don't tell your children how lonely you'll be— Christmas will be hard enough for them because you aren't there.

- If your finances are strained, and most people's are after a divorce, find inexpensive ways to have fun. Make snowmen, drink hot chocolate, snuggle up on the couch and watch a classic Christmas movie together.

- It's natural to be bitter and angry, but try to reframe your thinking. Instead of thinking about what you *don't* have, find ways to share what you *do* have. Visit a nursing home or bake cookies for a shelter.

- If you are the parent with more money, be sensitive to the fact that your former spouse may not have a lot to spend. Don't give overly extravagant gifts—help with winter clothing or other expenses instead.

- If your relationship with your ex-spouse allows, consider combining funds for an expensive item like a bike or a snowboard.

- Give gifts that help your child cope with going back and

forth between two households. Extra toiletry items, clothing, pajamas, toys, books, art supplies or an attractive comforter with a matching pillowcase will make both households feel like home.

- Buying kids' clothes can be a real challenge for single parents. If your family wants to give clothes for gifts, provide them with a list of the items and sizes needed. Encourage relatives to buy separates where practical—kids wear pants out much faster than other items. Dark colors don't show stains as quickly as lighter ones. Older children and teens may prefer a gift certificate for a particular store. If possible, buy unisex clothing that can be worn by an older child and then passed on to a sibling. A navy, gray, or dark green winter coat may be a better choice than a pink or purple one. You can always buy a hat and mitts in your child's favorite color to jazz it up. Encourage relatives to buy clothes that wash easily and don't need ironing. You have enough to do already.

- Don't be late picking your children up. If you are shopping or at a Christmas event, make sure you allow extra time for traffic. It's very stressful for children to sit waiting.

- If you won't be seeing your children at Christmas, mail or deliver your gifts early. Your child is counting on you!

Celebrating Christmas with a Blended Family

Christmas with a blended family can be extraordinarily difficult. Old angers, resentments, and conflicts can wreak havoc with carefully made plans. It takes time and tact to combine old traditions as you discover new ones. Have a family discussion about plans and expectations. Each person needs to express his or her feelings. Try to compromise where you can. If you expect some disharmony, you will be better prepared to deal with it. Holidays can be trigger points for emotional outbursts. Children grieve for a long time for the family, and the holiday, they used to have. Remember who is the grown up. Be patient. Give extra hugs.

- If you can afford to, consider spending Christmas somewhere new the first year. A place that has no family history for either part of your blended family is a better choice than one where either side has previously visited. Take lots of games and activities along.

- Ask your children which traditions they really want to bring to the new family. Even if it isn't the way you've always done it, it's important to incorporate some of their ideas. All children need the stability and comfort old traditions offer. Children in blended families need them even more, especially when they are finding their way in new relationships.

- Create some new traditions together—ordering pizza on Christmas Eve, going skating or making a wreath with boughs and pine cones collected on a family walk might be fun ones to begin with.

- Spend the same amount on gifts for each child. Make sure that the number of gifts children receive is also as even as possible. Children are quick to spot unfairness.

- Talk to grandparents about gifts. Perhaps they could give a family gift rather than individual presents, or all of the children might get a small gift such as a cozy sweatshirt or a pair of pajamas.

- Clear your calendar as much as possible to make time for family. People will understand when you explain that you have made a decision to spend more time at home together this year.

- If the two sets of children don't normally live together, try and find a bed for each or have all the kids camp out on sleeping bags in the family room. It's hard to be the kid who has to give up his/her bed and it's hard to be the kid whose "visitor status" is made very apparent because he/she doesn't have one. Bunk beds and roll away cots may help.

- If you hang stockings, make sure there is one for each child. Make ones for the kids who are coming as a family project.

- If everyone will be biking or skating, borrow or rent some equipment for the children coming for the holiday.

- Help the children make or buy small gifts for each other.

- If you are going to be including a family letter in your cards this year, ask *all* of the children to contribute a paragraph to it. If you send a picture, choose a photo that has *all* of you in it.

- If your children get along well, consider some joint gifts like board games. If you are just getting to know each other this year, find books or craft kits that will allow each child some private time during the holidays.

- Be sensitive when choosing Christmas movies the first year. Find funny ones neither set of children has seen before.

- If you have pictures of your children on display, make sure *both* sets of kids are equally represented.

- If your "in-house" children are very young, sharing toys can be difficult. Help them decide ahead of time which toys they feel they can share. Find a box with a lid to put the others in and put them in their closet to keep safe until after the holiday.

CHAPTER 11

Comfort and Joy

By Demitra B.,
age 8

"Blessed is the influence of one true loving human soul on another."
~ George Elliot

It is when we are ill that we are most in need of comfort, and of reassurance that our friends, despite the busyness of Christmas, have not forgotten us. Too often we find excuses to avoid visiting. We put it off because we are uncomfortable with illness, or we ask how we may help and then wait to be called. If someone you know is very ill, don't delay— think of something appropriate to do, and then *do* it! Small acts of kindness make difficult times more bearable, not only for the person who is ill, but for their spouse, children and caregivers. Here are some ways you can help:

- Call ahead to make arrangements. It's hard for sick people to do things spontaneously. Often they need to adjust their schedule in order to conserve their energy for your visit.

- Ask the person who is ill if there is anywhere special they would like to go during the Christmas season. Perhaps there is a special movie or a light display they'd like to see. Plan ahead, but be understanding if changes must be made.

- A trip to the hairdresser might be a welcome gift. Make arrangements to take your friend or arrange for a stylist to come to them.

- Go shopping together for a wig, a hat or a scarf for a very close friend who anticipates hair loss due to chemotherapy. Go out for lunch afterwards. Your moral support will be appreciated.

- Help make sure your friend or relative's Christmas outfit and those of their kids are ready. Drop off and pick up any clothes that need dry cleaning.

- Set aside two half days to help put up and take down your friend's Christmas tree.

- Put up and take down their outdoor lights.

- Take their children to a tree farm to choose a tree. Have lunch with the kids before or afterward.

- Make a cookie kit for their kids, complete with frozen or chilled dough, a tub of icing, sprinkles and cookie cutters. Set up a time to supervise the baking and decorating.

- Invite their children to your house for a baking or craft session so their mom or dad can have a nap.

- Give a pre-baked gingerbread house kit for Christmas. They are available at most large grocery chains. Help the kids put it together.

- Organize some friends, parents, or church members to bake an extra dozen of their favorite treat. Arrange an appropriate time to deliver the goodies.

- Ask your church group, neighbors, friends or school's parents to have a "freezer meal" blitz. Let the family receiving the meals know ahead of time to make sure freezer space will be available.

- Make a meal with all the fixings and drop it off on a night you've previously arranged.

- If you don't have time to cook, arrange to have a pizza delivered or pick up some pasta or roast chicken and a couple of salads at the grocery store.

- Videotape the Christmas concert for someone too ill to attend. Drive their children to and from the concert if necessary.

- Take their children to see Santa and pick up the photos afterward.

- Make a commitment to take their child to a sports event or club when you are driving your own kids. Skating lessons, hockey, swimming, Brownies and Cubs play a really important part in keeping the lives of the children involved as normal as possible under the cicumstances.

- Take your friend and their children for a drive to see the Christmas lights.

- Phone and ask if you can do some shopping for them when you are going to the mall.

- Offer to sit with a person who can't get out so their caregiver can have a rest or do some of their own Christmas shopping.

- Bring a terrific Christmas movie to your friend's house and watch it with them. Bring popcorn.

- A tape or CD of one of the "New Age" recordings of Christmas classics is a relaxing Christmas gift.

- Give their children snuggly toys for Christmas. Stuffed

animals can give a lot of comfort.

- Help wrap, deliver or mail their gifts.

- Help your friend with their cards if they wish to send them.

- Sometimes there are great financial hardships associated with illness. Find out discretely if your friend or family member needs help; if so, arrange to pay their electrical, phone or heating bill anonymously.

- If you live too far away to visit often, phone and send cards and letters with snapshots regularly.

- Encourage your children to make special cards to send.

- Buy a warm nighty or pajamas, snuggly slippers, or a collection of soothing herbal teas for a gift.

- Give a nicely-framed picture of your family to a close friend or relative who is in hospital.

- Decorate a relative's hospital room with a small wreath, a tiny tree or some colorful drawings from your children.

- For someone who will be in hospital Christmas Day, fill a stocking with tiny treats such as hand cream, a word search book, a favorite treat, some hard candies and a small bottle of cologne or aftershave.

- Too often we don't say the things closest to our hearts. Write a Christmas letter saying what you love, admire and cherish about your friend or relative.

- Make a very personalized pillow for your friend or relative to snuggle up with. Take your photo and a piece of plain, light-colored fabric to your local print shop. They can transfer it to the fabric. Frame the photo panel with an attractive print and sew it into a pillow.

- Often people are cold while having chemotherapy. It's easy to make a snuggly quilt with polar fleece. Just buttonhole stitch, zigzag or serge around the edges. Applique family members' handprints cut from different colored fleece. Wrap it up with a card that says, "Warm hugs from us to you."

- Give a photo album with pictures for Christmas this year.

- Make a special memory album for their children.

- Christmas can be very emotional for people who are ill. Give the gifts of your patience and understanding.

"Real friendship is shown in times of trouble;
prosperity is full of friends."
~ Euripides

Christmas and Alzheimer's

Relatives of family members with Alzheimer's also need your support at Christmas:

- Plan a very calm, quiet Christmas if you are spending it at home with an Alzheimer's patient. Too much excitement can be very distressing for them.

- Give simple-to-manage clothing for Christmas gifts. Tube socks, shoes with Velcro, and jogging outfits are easy to put on.

- Give materials to sort. Pennies and penny folders, a bag of buttons, nuts and bolts or large beads are good. A muffin tin makes a good sorting tray.

- Favorite songs often bring back special memories. Find suitable CD's or tapes or make your own.

- Take your friend or relative for a short car ride to see the lights. Take along another family member or friend to sit with them so you can concentrate on driving.

- Bake their favorite kind of Christmas cookie.

- Spend a few hours with the person needing care so the caregiver can do their Christmas shopping.

- Give the caregiver a gift certificate for a massage, a soothing bath basket, a book you know they'll enjoy or their favorite treat.

- Listen, really listen, to your caregiving friend. It is devastating to realize that their spouse, mother or father no longer recognizes them. Encourage them to use some of the support services available so they can have a break. Make a commitment to help whenever you can.

- If you are an out-of-town relative, find ways to support the family member who is doing the majority of the caregiving. Give up part of your holiday to ensure they get a much-needed rest. If you can afford to, arrange for someone to help with housework or yard maintenance.

Christmas and Grieving

When someone we love dies, holidays can be very painful. Reaching out to a friend or relative who has experienced a loss recently may be the best gift you give this year. Make a special point of visiting over the holidays. Bake some cookies and stop by for coffee—give lots of hugs. If you are trying to deal with loss, the following suggestions may help:

- Balance your family's needs with your own. Have a meeting to discuss what you would really like to do, as well as what you would prefer not to do, this year.

- Begin a new tradition or ritual that is meaningful for you such as lighting a special candle in memory of your loved one.

- Share your feelings with a friend or relative who is a good listener.

- Accept the help that is offered. If a good friend offers to help with baking, cleaning, or shopping or offers to look after your kids for an afternoon, let them help.

- Spend time with people who restore your spirits.

- This may be the year for a Christmas trip if you can afford it. If not, you may want to plan to visit friends or relatives on Christmas Day.

- After an emotional crisis, you'll be tired and need more "down time" over the holidays. Choose to do a few things that are really important, and let the others go this year. Skip sending cards or buy your baking if you wish. Give yourself permission to do less.

- If you have young children, use some of your vacation time to spend with them over the holidays this year; they will need your loving attention. If you can't arrange time off, perhaps grandma and grandpa, an aunt and uncle or a friend can spend some extra time with your kids.

- You may wish to have Christmas dinner at another family member's, a friend's house, or a restaurant. If you are staying at home, you may want to make small changes such as using a different tablecloth or dishes, changing the time of the meal or serving a buffet rather than a sit down meal.

- Try hard to do something for someone else this year. Help at a food bank, serve a meal to the homeless or pick out a toy for a needy child. It will help fill the void.

- If you can afford to, give a donation in memory of your loved one to a cause that would be meaningful for them.

- Select an ornament for each of your children or grand-children that represents something special about your loved one.

- When a much-loved teaching assistant died in our school district, her friends and colleagues decorated a tree for her teenaged daughter. Each person brought an angel ornament and read aloud a message about her mom as they placed their ornament on the tree. The messages were placed in an album for her daughter to read and re-read later on. The following December a candlelight walk was held in her memory. What a memorable tribute to a special person!

- Did you know you can name a star after a loved one? You can, and it can cost as little as $50. Contact the closest planetarium to inquire about naming a star. (The Pacific Space Centre in Vancouver has a great program.) You may want to give one to your own children or grandchildren or to the family of a friend. You might send a special card with an angel on it. Inside the card you could write, "Stars are the windows where angels peek through."

Kelsey's family went to the planetarium. They named a star after my mum. When I look at it I will feel a little bit sad and a little bit happy. By Aoife, 6

CHAPTER 12

An Animal Lover's Christmas

By Lauren C., age: 9

How Kids Can Help Animals
- get pets from the S.P.C.A.
- save some of your allowance
  to buy cat food and
  give it to the S.P.C.A.
- never ever abandon pets
  because they need you
- don't give pets chocolate
    by Molly C., age 8

If you are looking for a surefire way to get your kids involved in helping others at Christmas, pick a cause that involves animals. It can be especially good for children who need a little extra love themselves and can be a healing experience for their own hearts. It's easy to get started. Ask your local grocer if you can leave a decorated box by the exit doors for people to put pet food in when they are shopping. A group of children can organize a car wash or a penny drive and give the proceeds to an animal shelter or collect used towels and blankets to drop off. Here are some additional tips provided by animal-lovers and the S.P.C.A.:

- Don't give your children a pet for Christmas. There is too much going on at this time of year. Too many guests, excited children and potential hazards like Christmas trees and decorations make December an impractical time to bring home a frightened kitten or puppy. Instead, place a cuddly plush dog or cat under the tree or give a collar and leash for Christmas. Visit the shelter in January to choose your new family member.

- Decorate a jar and collect your change in order to make a donation to your local S.P.C.A. Help your children sort and count the coins.

- If your local grocery store or a big chain store allows you to donate your bonus points for shopping there to the S.P.C.A., do so. The shelter can use the points to buy staples like dog food.

- Pet shelters report they are always in need of these items: cat litter, dog food, dry cat chow, paper towels, Kleenex, bathroom tissue, bleach, canned cat food, dog leashes, dog and cat toys, animal carriers, collars, leashes, office supplies, towels and blankets, garbage bags and postage stamps. If you are able to give any of these supplies or cash, it will be greatly appreciated. Call ahead to see exactly what is needed. Take your child with you when you drop off your donation.

- Does your area have a wildlife recovery center? They are great places for family field trips. You may find you want to volunteer there. They also need many of the items requested by animal shelters.

- Make some items for your local S.P.C.A.'s Christmas bazaar. Use acrylic paint to make paw prints on the exterior of plastic bowls—add some doggie treats and tie the bowls up with cellophane! Make some car blankets from polar fleece for dogs and cats to snuggle up on. Cat and dog stockings and ornaments are always popular. Sew up some small fabric bags and fill them with dog biscuits or cat treats.

Make a Stocking for your cat!

by Brett M.
age 8

- Help your child make a stocking for your family pet. If you use felt and finish the edges with pinking shears, it's simple to do. A glitter glue pen makes it easy to add your pet's name. Take your child shopping to choose some small items to fill the stocking.

- Make a family commitment to walk dogs at your local animal shelter. Even once a month is helpful.

- If your cat or dog isn't spayed or neutered, make an appointment now for the New Year.

- Make or buy some muffins or cookies for the staff and volunteers at the S.P.C.A. These banana orange muffins are always popular and they are very healthy.

Stella's Banana Orange Muffins

3 cups bran
1 cup flour
1 cup raisins
1/2 cup wheat germ
2 tsp. baking soda
2 tsp. baking powder
1/2 tsp. salt
1/4 cup vegetable oil
1/4 cup molasses
1/2 cup liquid honey
1 1/3 cups milk
1 egg
1 large ripe banana
1 whole orange

In a large bowl, stir together bran, flour, raisins, wheat germ, baking soda, baking powder and salt. Pour oil, molasses, honey, milk, banana and egg into food processor or blender. Mix. Divide orange into eighths. Discard seeds only, drop the rest, including the peel, into the blender and blend til still slightly chunky. Pour liquid ingredients into dry ingredients.

Stir just enough to moisten. Spoon or scoop into 12 large or 18 medium greased muffin cups. Bake at 375°F for 15 to 20 minutes.

☆　☆　☆

- Give a book about birds and a bird feeder and birdseed. You can make bird feeders very easily by dipping pine cones in peanut butter and then rolling them in birdseed or by hollowing out half a grapefruit and filling it with birdseed. For a young carpenter, there are many well-made, reasonably priced birdhouse or bird feeder kits available.

Sarah J.
Age 8

Christmas on the Farm

Mooo-ing you a happy Christmas!

Ho Ho

Raymond J.
Age 12

- Decorate your tree after the holidays with bird friendly snacks like popcorn and leave it outside as a winter shelter for them.

- Read some of James Herriot's stories together. His stories for children include *The Christmas Kitten, Only One Woof* and *Moses the Kitten.* Dog lovers will enjoy his delightful collection of dog stories.

- For farming families and 4-H kids, here are some ideas from a young farmer for making Christmas on the farm extra special.

Christmas on the Farm

Christmas on the farm is special to me because our Christmas dinner is mostly homegrown. There is no big rush to get to the grocery store because we have most of it ready.

"Turkey day" is lots of fun. We start early in the morning and usually finish late at night. Everyone has a job. Lunch is always hot and hardy. By the time dinner time comes we all feel and smell like turkeys! Weighing the birds is exciting. Everyone likes to guess what the biggest turkey will be.

We always try to get ahead on the barn cleaning so that part is all taken care of for Christmas Day. We also like to have everything looking clean and tidy for when other farmers come to visit. They always want to see how the livestock is doing. We pay special attention to the show steers. They are well groomed and clipped ready for any visitors because we always want to show them off and have fun guessing weights and comparing hip and loin size with them. It's like playing "pick the winner."

The animals are always fed and taken care of before we have presents and brunch! I fork extra silage and say "Merry Christmas" to them all. Christmas music is on the barn radio because it plays 24 hours a day.

I always like to get and give farm stuff as presents. Last year I got a nice Western hat and a new grooming comb. Farm calendars are grabbed up quick. I like the ones with tractors.

Although I like school, being on the farm for the Christmas holiday is great fun for me.

By Raymond, T., farmer, age 12

CHAPTER 13

The Gift of a Green Planet

Help us take care of the world.

Tyler P. age 6

"Wishing you a world of gentleness and love where people give and care." ~ Anonymous

Christmas is not an environmentally sound holiday. We make lots of extra trips which produce extra emissions. Mountains of wrapping paper end up at the dump, and hundreds of thousands of unwanted gifts sit in our closets. The Center for a New American Dream reports that five million additional tons of trash are produced between Thanksgiving and New Year's. It's easy to make a few changes that can really make a difference—think of it as your gift to our planet, as well as to future generations.

- Plan your shopping so that you make as few trips as possible. Use the bus if you have good urban transit. Take a friend shopping so only one car is used; you'll enjoy spending time together while you shop. It will help reduce greenhouse gas emissions.

- Think carefully about the gift you are giving. Is it truly something the recipient wants or needs? My grandmother used to say, "Don't give old people something they have to dust. Food or a plant is better." You can't go wrong with a cheery poinsettia or a basket of warm muffins.

- Give food gifts such as a basket with all the ingredients for a pasta supper. Tuck in a couple of your most successful recipes.

- Recycle last year's cookie tins and baskets by filling them with newly baked or purchased cookies, bars, or muffins.

- If you don't have time to bake, fill mason jars from your local thrift store or recycling depot with the cookie mix-in-a-jar or brownie mix-in-a-jar recipes found in Chapter 18.

- Consider pooling your resources with other family members in order to give one really special gift. Most people have too much stuff and would be thrilled to get one item they really want.

- Give gifts that will last. Visit local craft fairs; you'll find lots of high quality items made from wood, stained glass, or hand-woven materials.

- Shop at antique stores and second-hand bookshops. You'll find wonderful treasures to delight even the most difficult to buy for person.

- If you are buying candles, choose those made from real beeswax. They are nontoxic and don't give off fumes that can aggravate allergies.

- Take along your own shopping bags. Reasonably priced lightweight muslin bags are available at many stores. Give a couple of bags to an environmentally conscious friend for Christmas.

- Use wrapping materials you already have in the house. Scraps of material can be sewn into re-usable bags. Brown paper bags can be cut apart, turned inside out and stamped with gold paint. Add some raffia and a piece of cedar bough for an elegant package.

- Use sturdy gift bags which can be recycled several times.

- Use recycled Christmas cards for tags.

- Reuse ribbon—if we all recycled just a couple of feet each year, we could tie a bow around our planet.

- Use your extra photos as gift tags—the recipients will love them!

- Make your own wreath from natural items rather than purchasing a plastic one. Buy or make a loosely woven grapevine wreath and tuck lots of cedar or fir boughs between the twigs. Wire on some pine cones and a big bow. Wreaths make wonderful, inexpensive, environmentally sound gifts. (Save the grapevine base to reuse next year.)

- Use natural materials like cedar boughs and pine cones to decorate with. They can be used for mulch or compost after the holidays are over.

- Give a savings bond. There's no wrapping and no waste.

- Real gingerbread cookies make lovely, edible decorations. Before baking, insert a small tube cut from a paper straw through the top of each cookie so you'll have a hole to thread a ribbon through.

- Use cloth napkins and washable plates rather than disposable paper products.

- Recycle plastic beverage containers and tin cans.

- When you are shopping, buy the largest size practical in order to reduce excess packaging. Shop in the bulk food section.

- Give gifts to children that DON'T require batteries but DO require imagination.

- Popped popcorn makes a great packing product to protect breakables when shipped. Put a note in asking the recipient to feed it to the birds after opening your gift.

- Turn off your Christmas lights whenever you can, not only as a safety precaution, but to reduce electrical consumption.

- For the person who has everything, consider giving a gift certificate for a course related to their favorite hobby. Your local college's continuing education program probably offers courses in computer skills, gardening, cooking, astrology or genealogy.

- Take the kids for a walk or hike outside during your holiday. Look at the wildlife or stars. Reflect on the miracles of nature.

- Give books to children and adults alike about wildlife, nature, ecology, and gardening.

- Give your children or your school's library a good book about recycling projects for kids.

- After Christmas, help start a club at school for kids who care about our planet. The Canadian (or American) Wildlife Federation has all the materials you need, and they're free.

- Give a gift that gives twice by purchasing your cards, calendars or gifts from an environmental organization or nature center. You can contact The Canadian Wildlife Federation or The National Wildlife Federation in the U.S. Both are easy to access through the Internet. Just do a search under their names.

- Some communities will pick up Christmas trees and use them for mulch in parks or playgrounds.

- Before or after Christmas, donate unwanted items to a non-profit organization that supports environmental projects.

- If you are tired of buying gifts which seem to be unwanted or unneeded, or you are just plain broke, make a coupon and tuck it in a beautiful Christmas card. You can offer help with housework, babysitting, cooking, or snow shoveling. When Christmas is over, make sure you honor your promises.

- Make a coupon that entitles the bearer to homemade baking once a month for an entire year. This is a gift that is especially appreciated by seniors, who will look forward to your visit as much as your baking. That sounds like a lot, but it's easy to make a few extra muffins or cookies when you are baking some for your own family. Arrange the treats attractively on a plate and add a seasonal decoration such as a paper heart for Valentine's Day. Pumpkin muffins would be great in October. Irish soda bread is simple to make in March.

Irish Soda Bread

2 cups whole wheat flour
2 cups white flour
2 tsp. baking powder
1 tsp. baking soda
1 egg
1 1/2 cups buttermilk
2 tbsp. syrup (any kind)

Combine dry ingredients. Combine wet ingredients. Mix both together until dough lets go of side of bowl. Knead 5 or 6 times on a floured counter. Shape into a round loaf on a baking sheet. Score the loaf with a few lines and bake at 375°F for 50 to 60 minutes.

·☆· ·☆· ·☆·

- Give carpentry lessons to a youngster. Help them make something simple such as coasters, a trivet or a garden ornament.

- Teach a child to crochet or knit. A ball of yarn, a crochet hook, and a coupon for lessons with you is an easy, inexpensive gift, especially if you are a senior on a fixed income.

- Take a tin of cookies or some fresh donuts to the recycling depot staff. They work hard, and would love to be acknowledged!

- These cookies make a fantastic gift. They are absolutely sensational.

Truly Decadent Chocolate Chip Cookies

1/2 cup unsalted butter (at room temperature)
3/4 cup packed dark brown sugar
1/4 cup white sugar
1 tsp. vanilla
1/4 tsp. salt
1/3 cup chunky peanut butter
1 egg
1/2 tsp. baking soda
1 cup flour
3/4 cup coarsely chopped unsalted roasted peanuts
2 cups semisweet chocolate chips

Preheat oven to 350°F. Grease the cookie sheets. In a large mixing bowl, cream the butter with the brown sugar, white sugar, vanilla and salt. Beat until fluffy. Beat in the peanut butter, egg, and soda. Stir in the flour and then add the peanuts and chocolate. Mix well. Put into a smaller bowl and chill for at least four hours or overnight. Use 2 or 3 tbsp. of dough for each cookie. Shape into balls. Leave at least three inches between cookies.

Bake for 10 to 12 minutes (until the cookie springs back when lightly touched). Don't overbake. Cool for 2 minutes on cookie sheets before transferring to a rack. Makes 20-32 large cookies.

Wish list for The World

- save trees

- everyone would recycle

- make peace on Earth

- a cleaner world

- no hunting animals just
  for fun

- save the poor
  by Quinn H., age 8

CHAPTER 14

Celebrating With Books

by William S.
age 8

I love the book The Best
Christmas Pageant Ever

One of the most important gifts you can give your children is the love of good literature. Kids who love to read are seldom bored—a book can be their best friend on a rainy day or a long trip. Reading new books and re-reading old favorites should become an important part of your family's Christmas celebration. Of the hundreds of new Christmas books published each year, a few will join the ranks of the classics. When you are tired and frazzled, turn on the Christmas tree lights and snuggle up with a great book on the sofa together.

Books are also meant for sharing. Consider giving a book to your children's school library as a Christmas gift. The librarian often has a list of books he/she would like to purchase but may not be able to afford because of budget restrictions. If your school doesn't have a program to encourage families to donate a book, help the librarian start one. If you see good books which are reasonably priced at a markdown sale or a garage sale, pick some up to donate to a family shelter, daycare, or children's hospital. All children need good books, and kids in distress need the comfort of being read to even more. Don't forget to include a chapter book for older children too.

- Read *The Night Before Christmas*, by Clement Moore, with your family every Christmas Eve.

- *A Child's Christmas in Wales*, by Dylan Thomas, is a wonderful addition to your Christmas library.

Every Christmas, starting about a week before the twenty-fifth, my dad reads the family A Christmas Carol by Charles Dickens. Some years we end up by reading the whole book in one sitting. This normally means we just start again the next night. It's such a wonderful story that it makes us all smile and cry by turns.
By Tara Phillips, age 21

- Read Barbara Robinson's *The Best Christmas Pageant Ever* aloud together. You'll laugh til you cry. Pick up a couple of extra copies to give to your children's Sunday school teacher, favorite aunt, grandparents, cousins, or special friends.

- If you want a book that will encourage your children to consider the needs of the homeless but is sensitively written for youngsters, try Natalie Savage Carlson's *The Family Under the Bridge*. Afterwards, think of a family project that will help the homeless in your community.

- Beginning readers love Lillian Hoban's "Arthur" series. Try *Arthur's Christmas* or *Arthur's Christmas Cookies*.

- A perennial favorite for seven to ten year-olds is Laura Ingalls Wilder's *Christmas in the Big Woods*.

- Susan Korman's book, *Annabelle's Wish*, encourages caring and generosity.

- The *Velveteen Rabbit* with its timeless message of the power of love makes a lovely Christmas gift.

- Margaret Wise Brown's books have brought comfort to children and parents alike for over fifty years. Look for two classics, *The Runaway Bunny* and *Goodnight Moon*; they're terrific gifts for pre-schoolers.

- Robert Munsch's *Love You Forever* is a fantastic gift for parents with a new baby. Kids up to nine love the humor and sound effects in his other zany books.

- Look for books by Jan Brett; her illustrations are exquisite. Kindergarten to Grade Three children love

The Mitten, The Hat, The Wild Christmas Reindeer, and *The Trouble With Trolls.*

- Children under six love "lift the flap" books like the "Nicky" series by Harriet Zieffert and the "Spot" books by Eric Hill.

- If your child isn't a fiction reader, and some kids aren't, shop for books that match his or her interests. There are lots of easy-to-read science books about dinosaurs, lizards, volcanoes, motorcycles and bugs.

Other ways to encourage more reading in your home are to:

- Ask some of your guests to read a Christmas story to your children. Children need to see lots of people model reading.

- Encourage older kids who are reluctant readers to take turns reading with you, each reading a chapter on alternate nights. Look for the books that have won the Newbery Medal—the anthology entitled *A Newbery Christmas* is excellent. Your librarian can help you find more great stories.

- Give gift certificates to bookstores as gifts to your children, nieces, nephews and older relatives.

- Give subscriptions to magazines like *Owl, Chickadee* or National Geographic's *World* to children. Your gift will keep coming all year.

- Collect Christmas books to bring out each December 1st. Read a different story each night. Supplement your own collection by visiting the library.

- When planning your shopping, don't forget babies need books too. Look for sturdy "board books." Counting books and ABC books are a hit with younger children.

- Older children can tape a story to give along with a book for younger relatives. They should practice reading the book several times first in order to develop fluency and expression. Remember to tell the listener when to turn the page.

- Don't be too quick to give away books once your children have heard them a couple of times. Children love to re-read old favorites as their own reading ability grows. Ones that you might consider too easy can be read to younger siblings or small visitors.

- Visit your local library and get an application for your child's library card. Roll it up and tie it with colorful ribbon. Tuck it into his or her stocking.

- Get to know the children's librarian in your local library as well as a salesclerk or owner in your favorite bookstore. They have a wealth of information to share with you about the best fiction and non-fiction books for children. If they've been very helpful, buy or bake some cookies as a thoughtful thank you.

Sharing Books

- Set up a donation box for gently-used books at your school, gym, or office. Collect children's books or pocket books for a hospital or shelter.

- Host a book trading party for children or adults. Ask each guest to bring several books to trade.

- Volunteer to teach an adult to read. It's a terrific way to make a real difference in someone's life, and you may make a new friend!

- Collect books or cash donations for a school or daycare center that really needs them.

- Drop off copies of current magazines at your local hospital when you've finished reading them.

- Give a children's magazine subscription to the pediatric ward at your hospital.

- If your school uses one of the book club programs such as Scholastic, consider donating some of the bonus books to an organization that needs them.

- Children also need lots of opportunities to write; put pens, stickers and tiny blank notebooks in their stockings.

- Use family photos to illustrate your own books. Make an extra copy to give to Grandma!

- Write your own family version of *The Night Before Christmas.*

- Make a counting book for a younger family member, friend, or cousin. Use photos, your own drawings, recycled Christmas cards or pictures from magazines as illustrations.

- Help your children write a letter to their favorite author.

Send it to the publisher's address inside the front of the book. Maybe they'll write back, but even if they don't, authors love receiving mail from young fans.

- Give "how to" books along with the necessary supplies to project-oriented kids who are not generally readers.

- Make visiting the library as often as the video store a priority for your family in the New Year.

"When I... discovered libraries,
it was like having Christmas every day."
~ Jean Fritz

CHAPTER 15

Remembering Seniors at Christmas

By Talissa K., 10

Last year the class made
Candy sleighs for Meals on Wheels
and gave them to old people.
After Christmas an old lady sent
me a thank you card. I felt so
happy I shared it with everyone. I
loved it.

By Jessica. L., age 8

"I miss having someone to love and having someone who loves me. I miss seeing children, and hearing them laugh."
~ Elsie W., nursing home resident

We used to grow up in close contact with our grandparents, aunts, uncles, cousins and elderly neighbors. Unfortunately, that isn't as true today. Many grandchildren live hundreds of miles away from their grandparents; most of us don't know our older neighbors at all. Whether your kids are five or fifteen, they can benefit from spending time with older relatives or from making friends with seniors. You might begin by reading Tom Hegg's marvelous book, *A Christmas Cup of Tea* or his sequel, *A Memory of Christmas Tea* with your children over the holidays. Then plan some acts of "Christmas kindness" yourselves.

Christmas at the Seniors' Residence

Residents in seniors' homes love to see young families in December or anytime throughout the year. Call ahead to arrange a suitable time. Ask the director for the names of residents who seldom get visitors and make a special point of spending a few minutes with them.

- Encourage your children to prepare for the visit by baking homemade cookies, making cards or drawing Christmas pictures.

- Ask the activity director if you and your children could help with a craft session. After helping once, you could arrange to bring an idea of your own along with the necessary materials. Many of the crafts that children enjoy are suitable for older people too.

- Take your children and a musical friend along to play the piano while you sing.

- A Guide or Scout troop can provide a wrapping station for seniors. Make sure the date and time are advertised so residents can have their presents ready. Ask each child to bring a different item—you'll need tags, wrap, ribbon, bows and lots of tape. Ask the children to bring their supplies a week earlier so you can check you have everything you need. Make your own gift-wrap and tags ahead of time if you wish, or simply use store-bought materials. Foil is easier to wrap with. Practice wrapping ahead of time.

- Pot up a tiny tree in a four or six-inch clay pot for a relative living in a nursing home. Make an extra one for the nursing station. If you are working with a large group of children, make one for each dining room table. You can paint the pot or leave it plain. Dark green paint or burgundy paint with a gold rim looks great! A light color like off-white is also effective if you want the children to write Christmas messages on the pots with colored permanent felts. An adult should spray the pot with a clear acrylic sealer in a well-ventilated area.

   Now you are ready to add a tiny tree. If you are in the woods, look for a very small tree growing beneath a larger one—it won't survive because it can't get enough light. If working with a large number of children, you could ask a local forestry company to donate seedlings. You can buy tiny wrapped boxes to place under the tree at a craft store. Add some miniature garland and tiny ornaments. Seniors will be delighted by the children's thoughtful gift.

- Offer to spend a few hours mending residents' clothing so they'll feel well dressed for the holidays. It's a worthwhile project for a home-economics teacher's senior students to undertake.

- Ask for the name of someone who seldom receives mail and send seasonal cards for a whole year. Seniors especially enjoy the ones made by children.

- A good project for a class at school or a Brownie or Cub troop is to make some small decorations to fit on the residents' trays for Christmas dinner. You could also purchase plain white paper placemats for the children to decorate for tables or trays. Provide some sparkly glitter glue so the children can dress their drawings up!

Brownies can help older people at Christmas. We can make little gifts for them. We could make a wreath. We could decorate a little tree for them. We could bake a cake or cookies for them.

by Morganne B, age 7

- Encourage an older child to be a reading buddy for someone who has lost his or her sight. If time allows, make it a long-term commitment. If not, volunteer for an afternoon and take along some Christmas short stories to share. Your local library can assist with selections and women's magazines are also a good source of Christmas stories. Make sure your child rehearses the reading material first in order to develop confidence.

- Make some simple stockings. Collect small items like candy and toiletries at your church or school to fill them up with and donate the stockings to residents without family.

- Bake gingerbread men or fancy cookies to decorate trays. This can be a family or group project. It's also fun for home-ec classes.

- Make corsages for the ladies. It's not really very hard to do. Baste gathering stitches along a 12-inch piece of flat lace and gather it into a circle. Glue a satin bow and a fabric flower on. Make boutonnieres with artificial Christmas greenery for the gentlemen. Attach large safety pins rather than corsage pins—they are much easier for arthritic hands to fasten.

- Arrange for your school or church's band or choir to play carols. Bring along cards or decorations to give the audience. If your group is too busy at Christmas, and many choirs are, arrange to visit near Valentine's Day instead and bring valentines to pass out to the residents.

- If you have a relative in a nursing home, help your children make a special card for the staff thanking them for taking good care of their grandma or grandpa. Bake or buy some cookies for the staff's coffee break.

- Organize a big buddy, little buddy program where a Brownie or Cub troop or a class becomes special friends with a group of seniors. They can exchange letters and get together for special days.

- Make paper plate wreaths to decorate residents' doors.

- Make a felt banner for your special senior's room. Use lots of sequins and glitter—children love working with sparkly stuff. It's easy to do with a good tacky craft glue and some simple felt shapes cut from cookie cutters.

- An ideal project for an older group of kids or teens is to make tote bags, cushions or lap quilts for seniors. Look on the Internet for sewing project ideas or ask your local quilt guild to join you in making this project more successful.

Closer to Home

Perhaps you have an elderly neighbor who would welcome your visits or help:

- Prepare several containers of homemade soup along with small packages of buns for your elderly neighbor or relative. If you have a bread machine, it's easy to make fresh buns. If not, pick up half a dozen at your favorite bakery. Here is a hearty, nutritious soup recipe.

Meal-in-a-Soup

1 tsp. butter or margarine
1 lb. hamburger or ground turkey
2 medium onions, finely chopped
1 medium potato, peeled and diced (omit if freezing soup)
1 1/4 cups cauliflower flowerets or any other vegetables you want to use up
1/2 cup finely chopped carrot
1-19 oz. can diced tomatoes or 2 cups chopped fresh tomatoes
1 1/2 tsp. salt
1/8 tsp. pepper
6 cups water
3/4 cup macaroni or small shell pasta

Melt butter in large pot. Add hamburger or turkey and brown slightly. Add all remaining ingredients except the pasta. Cover and bring to a boil. Reduce heat and simmer 30 minutes. Add pasta and cook for another 10 minutes. Garnish with Parmesan cheese before serving. Makes approximately 12 cups.

- Make a commitment to shovel an elderly neighbor's walk while school is out over the holidays. If possible, continue doing so throughout the snowy season. Working alongside your child will make it more fun!

- Do a little extra baking to share with an older friend.

- Ask someone who is homebound if you can help with his or her Christmas shopping when you are going to the mall.

- Make arrangements to drop off and pick up a neighbor who no longer drives when you are going shopping.

- Help compose a Christmas letter for a neighbor who finds it hard to write. Photocopy it and address their envelopes.

- Help put up their outdoor lights. Set a date to take them down too, and mark it on your calendar.

- Arrange to pick up an extra live tree or help put up their artificial one. Again, be available to help take it down after Christmas.

- Invite an elderly person for Christmas tea or take a tea party to them!

- Invite someone you know will be alone to come for Christmas dinner. If they are housebound, fix a plate of turkey and all the trimmings and assign the role of delivery person to one of your teenagers or guests.

- Phone an elderly neighbor just to say hello on a regular basis.

We should be nice
to old people because
they are old and they are
going soon.

Billy M.
8 years old

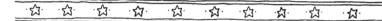

CHAPTER 16

With Love From Grandma and Grandpa

Chantal, 6

Can Grandma come out to play?

What children really need from grandparents is not lots of presents, but a close relationship throughout the year. Today's grandparents are pretty busy, but it's important for them to make time to reach out to the younger generation. Don't feel you have to spend a lot of money on gifts—the most important one is spending time with you! Give your grandchildren lots of hugs and keep hugging them when they are teenagers!

Here are some terrific ways for grandparents to develop close, loving relationships with grandchildren:

- Teach them to bake. Kids of all ages enjoy cooking. If you don't, use frozen cookie dough and decorate the cookies together. The memories and time together are more important than the recipes.

- Are you a long-distance grandparent who would love to be able to read to your grandchild? Visit a bookstore that specializes in children's literature. The staff will be able to recommend good books to read aloud. Make a tape and send it along with the book for a unique gift. Practice first, but don't focus on perfection; your grandchildren will love hearing your voice.

- Phone on the first snowy day and ask if anyone would like to come for hot chocolate and a snowman building session. If you can't be together, make up a snowman kit with some buttons, a scarf, a hat, and some twigs for arms. Mail it to your grandchildren early in December.

- Set aside a day to serve your grandchildren their favorite lunch or to take them to a restaurant. Afterwards, take them to a Christmas play or movie.

- Invite the grandchildren for a weekend so their mom and dad can get organized for Christmas. If you are on a limited budget, this can be your gift to your son or daughter.

- Make a video to send to grandbabies that you don't get to see often. Visit your library and borrow a book with fingerplays and simple songs for babies. You may feel a little silly singing lullabies or playing peekaboo—using a hand puppet helps.

- Take lots of pictures when you are with your grand-children. Make an album with captions to accompany each photograph. Make sure that you are in some of the pictures too! Give one copy as a gift and keep another for yourself.

- Phone your grandchildren at least once a week. Long distance phone plans make it very reasonable to talk often.

- Send a special card or letter to each grandchild often. Children love getting mail. Give them a special box to save your letters to them in!

- Write down your favorite Christmas memories from when you were a child, a teen, a new parent and a grandparent, and send each of your children a copy to share with their children.

- Teach a skill like woodworking or crocheting to your grandchild. Remember to be patient and encouraging; the process is more important than the product. Whether or not the project turns out is not as important as the closeness you develop.

- Ask an older child to give you computer lessons for your Christmas present. You will be amazed at what they can teach you when you haven't even found the on switch yet! Ask them to teach you how to e-mail.

- Start a collection for your grandchildren. Choose something inexpensive like buttons, stamps, shells or postcards. Give one of your nicest teacups to a granddaughter to begin a collection.

My gramma taught me how to Knit. I Know how to make scarves and my mom Knows how to make mittens and socks and stockings.

by clara B., age 7

- Build a wooden chest or jewelry box for a teenaged granddaughter as a special keepsake.

- No grandchildren close by? Invite a young family to come for a cup of Christmas tea and cookies. You'll enjoy their excitement.

Going to Grandma
and Grandpa's house.

by Stewart S., age 8

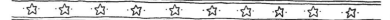

CHAPTER 17

Sharing the Joys of Cooking

Annie S., Age 10

I love my Mother's baking.
I love it when she takes
the cookies fresh from the oven.
I love smelling the sweet smell.
I love rolling the dough
and feeling the texture.
But... most of all I love
tasting her peanut butter
cookies.

by Carly B.,
age 9

·☆· ·☆· ·☆·

My grandmother was a truly exceptional cook. Her lemon pie was so good that people would line up an hour early for church suppers hoping to get a piece. She believed that children needed to be actively involved in Christmas preparations, so from the time I was six or seven, we would begin baking together late in November. At first my role consisted of choosing which cookie cutters to use and putting lots of icing and sprinkles on the sugar cookies. While we baked, we talked about her Christmases as a youngster at home. She told of the pen wipers and hankies that she sewed for gifts. She loved to tell me about her six brothers and sisters and their favorite Christmas dishes, which included bread pudding with caramel sauce, carrot pudding, butter tarts and "ice box" cookies.

The phrase "quality time" had not been invented yet, but that is what our time together was. We enjoyed each other's company while she shared the irreplaceable gift of her memories. She loved music and taught me many of the marvelous songs popular in the early years of the 1900's. Later on, when her hands were crippled by arthritis, it was my turn to mix and knead while she supervised. Each Christmas, I use many of her recipes. In my heart, I still hear her rich alto voice singing.

You too can create a wealth of warm memories with your children or grandchildren when you cook together. You'll find lots of simple but successful recipes in this chapter for children and adults alike to try. Give some as gifts—baking is never the wrong size or color.

Gifts for Cooks

- Give a child a set of cookie cutters, an apron, and a cookbook. Add a coupon indicating how many cooking sessions you will help them with.

- A basket of cookie cutters, a rolling or springerle pin, an icing bag and tips, a cake tester, a candy thermometer, or some of those wonderful insulated cookie sheets would be appreciated by the baker on your list.

- A new cook can always use kitchen scissors, a set of measuring cups, a kitchen timer, or a basic cookbook.

- Wrap up a new wire whisk with some chocolate kisses and a tag that says "We whisk you a Merry Christmas, with lots of hugs and kisses."

- Don't know what to give a teen? Compile a special cookbook of family recipes to use when they move out on their own. Ask their grandparents, aunts and uncles to contribute recipes too. Copy them neatly on file cards to give in an attractive recipe box.

- If you've been involved in making a cookbook at work or school, order extra copies to give your children when they are older.

- If an older relative or friend needs help compiling a collection of their recipes for their children or grand-children volunteer to type them up and have copies made.

Christmas Recipes

If you need an easy treat for a cookie exchange, these tarts are truly fabulous. If you are short of time, buy pre-made shells.

Best Ever Butter Tarts

1/3 cup butter
1/2 cup golden syrup
1/2 cup golden sugar
1/2 to 2/3 cup raisins or currants
1/2 tsp. vanilla
1/4 tsp. salt
2 eggs (use only one egg for very syrupy filling)

Line 12 3-inch tart cups with pastry. Chill while you are making the filling. Melt the butter in a medium-sized pan and add all of the ingredients except the egg. Mix well. Let the mixture cool, then add the egg, beaten just enough to combine the yolk and the white. Pour the filling into the pastry-lined tins and bake on the lowest rack in a 450°F oven for 15 to 20 minutes. Once baked, loosen the edges with a pointed knife and let stand at least 10 minutes before removing from tins.

Cream Cheese Sugar Cookies

I've used this recipe very successfully with my kindergarten and primary students for many years. Kids love to decorate sugar cookies, and these are really easy to roll. You can make the dough one day and bake the next or you can freeze the dough for a few weeks.

1 cup white sugar
1 cup butter
3 oz. softened cream cheese
1/2 tsp. almond extract
1/2 tsp. vanilla
1 egg yolk
2 3/4 cups flour

Combine butter, cream cheese and egg yolk. Beat until fluffy, by hand or with a mixer. Add sugar very gradually. Continue beating. Blend in vanilla and almond extract. Mix in the flour gradually. Dough should be chilled for at least 1 hour. Preheat oven to 375°F. Roll out dough on a lightly floured board until 1/8th of an inch thick, using one third at a time. Cut out. Bake on an ungreased cookie sheet for 7 to 10 minutes. Makes several dozen, depending on the size of your cookie cutters.

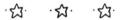

Lemon Bars

The tart lemon flavor of these bars is always appreciated —they make a superb gift or a delicious addition to a buffet table. And best of all, you usually have all the ingredients you need to bake them on hand.

2 cups flour
1 cup butter
1/2 cup icing sugar
1/2 tsp. salt
4 eggs, beaten
2 cups sugar
1/2 tsp. baking powder
4 tsp. flour
5 tbsp. fresh lemon juice
rind of 1 lemon, grated

Cream the flour, butter, icing sugar and salt together until crumbly. Pat down gently into a greased 9" x 13" pan. Bake 20 minutes at 325°F. Combine remaining ingredients and pour over the hot crust. Bake 25 minutes more. Remove from oven and sprinkle with sifted icing sugar. Cool and then cut with a wet knife.

·☆· ·☆· ·☆·

• Make some gingerbread men to give to your friends, for your children's classrooms, for a seniors' center, or your local Meals on Wheels program. A local women's shelter or your local soup kitchen's lunch program would love to receive some too. A small tree covered with gingerbread ornaments makes a great raffle prize for an organization wishing to raise money. A wreath decorated with cookies makes a great second prize.

Easy Gingerbread Cookies

one package (6 serving size) of regular butterscotch pudding and pie filling mix
3/4 cup margarine
3/4 cup brown sugar
1 egg
2 1/4 cups regular flour
1 tsp. baking soda
3 tsp. ginger
2 tsp. cinnamon

Cream pie filling mix with margarine and sugar. Add egg and blend well. Combine flour, baking soda, ginger and cinnamon and blend into pudding mixture. Chill dough until firm—at least 10 minutes. Roll on floured board to 1/4 inch thickness and cut shapes out with cookie cutters. Place on greased baking sheets. Bake at 350°F for 10 to 12 minutes. Cool on wire rack and decorate as desired.

Christmas Caramels

2 cups light corn syrup
1 lb. brown sugar
1 can sweetened condensed milk
1/2 lb. butter
1 cup nuts

An adult or responsible teen should be in charge of the stove as the syrup gets very hot! Mix the first four ingredients together. Simmer, stirring continuously, until mixture reaches the soft ball stage (240°F). Add nuts and pour into a well-buttered pan. Let cool and then refrigerate. After the mixture is very firm, cut it into small squares with an oiled knife. Wrap each one in wax paper. For a fancier presentation, rewrap the squares in colored foil.

☆ ☆ ☆

Marble Bark

Another easy to prepare gift is homemade almond bark.

6 squares bittersweet chocolate
6 squares white chocolate
1 cup toasted whole almonds

Carefully microwave each chocolate separately on medium power until melted. Stir half of the nuts into each bowl. Spoon the chocolate mixtures onto a wax paper lined cookie sheet. Use a knife to gently marble the two types of chocolate and refrigerate until firm. Put the bark in a plastic bag and tie it up with curly ribbon to tuck into an inexpensive gift bag lined with tissue.

☆ ☆ ☆

Cherry Pineapple Squares

This recipe is one of my grandmother's very best. Surprisingly, it doesn't require a lot of sugar. It may sound a little fussy, but is well worth the effort. The cherries and pineapple are very colorful and the meringue looks like a blanket of snow.

Base:
2 cups flour
1 cup butter
2 tbsp. sugar
pinch of salt

Filling:
1-14 ounce can of crushed pineapple, undrained
1/4 cup sugar
2 tbsp. cornstarch
1/4 cup cold water
3/4 cup chopped, well drained, maraschino cherries

Topping:
4 egg whites
2 tbsp. sugar
3/4 to 1 tsp. almond extract
1 cup fancy coconut (optional)

Mix the base ingredients together until very crumbly, and pat mixture into a greased 9" x 13" glass pan. Bake at 325°F for 15 minutes or until lightly golden.

Meanwhile, put the pineapple in a saucepan. Add the sugar, and then add the cornstarch, which has been mixed with the cold water. Add the cherries, and bring to a boil. Cook until thickened and clear and spread over the base.

Beat the egg whites as you do for a meringue, slowly adding the sugar. Add the flavoring and coconut and spread it over the pineapple and cherry layer. Bake at 400°F until meringue is a golden brown. Watch very carefully, it only takes 3 to 5 minutes. Cool, then cut into squares.

·☆· ·☆· ·☆·

Aunt Trudy's Heart Smart Gingersnaps

A batch of these "heart-smart cookies" makes a great gift for anyone watching their cholesterol. Collect tins throughout the year at garage sales. Copy the recipe on a Christmas card to enclose with a couple of dozen cookies.

2 1/4 cups flour
1 cup (packed) brown sugar
3/4 cup canola oil
1/4 cup molasses
1 tsp. baking soda
1 tsp. ginger
1 tsp. cinnamon
1/2 tsp. cloves
1 egg
1/4 cup white sugar

Place half of the flour in a large bowl. Add the brown sugar, egg, baking soda, and spices, and mix well. Add the molasses slowly and beat with an electric mixer til thoroughly mixed. Beat or stir in the remaining flour. Shape dough in 1 inch balls and roll them in white sugar. Place 2 inches apart on ungreased cookie sheet. Bake 8 to 10 minutes at 375°F until edges set and top crackles. Cool for a minute on cookie sheets and then on racks. Makes 48 cookies.

☆ ☆ ☆

Chocolate Sour Cream Banana Cake

If you have a "hard to buy for" teenager on your list, you could bake this cake to wrap up along with a good beginner's cookbook.

1 cup butter or margarine
2 cups white sugar
2 large eggs
1 tsp. vanilla
3 cups mashed bananas
2 tsp. baking powder
2 tsp. baking soda
3 cups flour
1 cup dairy sour cream
1/2 cup brown sugar
1 tsp. ground cinnamon
1 1/2 cups chocolate chips

Cream together butter and white sugar. Add eggs, one at a time, beating well after each addition. Add vanilla and mashed bananas. Combine flour, baking powder, and baking soda; add to banana mixture alternately with sour cream, ending with dry ingredients. Spoon and spread half the batter into a well-greased 9" x 13" glass pan. Combine cinnamon and brown sugar. Sprinkle remaining half of this mixture over the batter in the pan. Top with half of the chocolate chips. Repeat layers. Bake at 350°F for 50 to 60 minutes.

This cake is very moist, keeps well in the fridge, and freezes beautifully.

☆ ·☆· ·☆·

Mom's Morning Glory Muffins

These moist, fruit-filled muffins are great to serve Christmas morning along with a fruit salad. Put some in an attractive basket you've lined with a square of Christmas fabric for a welcome gift.

1 1/4 cups white sugar
2 1/4 cups flour
1 tbsp. cinnamon
2 tsp. baking soda
1/4 tsp. salt
1/2 cup shredded coconut
1/2 cup raisins
2 cups grated carrot
1 apple, shredded
8 ounces drained, crushed pineapple
1/2 cup walnuts or pecans
3 large eggs
1 cup canola oil
1 tsp. vanilla

Sift the sugar, flour, cinnamon, baking soda and salt together into a large bowl. Add the fruit, carrots, and nuts. Stir to combine. In a separate bowl, whisk the eggs with the oil and vanilla. Pour this mixture into the bowl with the dry ingredients and blend well. Spoon into 16 cupcake tins which have been lined with muffin liners. Fill each cup to the brim.

Bake in a preheated 350ºF oven for 35 minutes or until a toothpick inserted in the center of a muffin comes out clean. Cool in the pan for 10 minutes, then turn out onto a rack. These muffins freeze or keep well.

☆   ☆   ☆

Are you tired of doing all the work for the Christmas meal? Assign everyone in the family one part to prepare. Little ones can help tear the bread for the stuffing; older ones can help with the salad. You'll love both of these recipes.

☆   ☆   ☆

Moist Whole Wheat Raisin Stuffing

1 large onion
1 cup chopped celery
1 cup butter or margarine
16 cups fresh brown bread crumbs
1 cup dark raisins
1 cup chopped walnuts (optional)
1 tsp. salt and pinch of pepper
1 cup chopped apple
1 to 2 tbsp. poultry seasoning or thyme and sage mixed equally
1 chicken bouillon cube
1 cup of hot water

Put your children to work tearing the fresh bread into chunks while you chop the celery. Using the tops as well, saute celery along with the onion in butter. Pour the melted butter or margarine along with the onion and celery over the bread. Add the raisins, nuts and apples and toss well.

Sprinkle with seasonings. (I prefer the sage and thyme mixture to the premixed poultry seasoning.) Dissolve the chicken cube in hot water, and sprinkle the liquid over the dressing. Mix well. This stuffs a 20 pound turkey easily, but extra dressing can be baked in a casserole. Always moist and delicious, this stuffing could become a family legend.

Christmas Orange Salad

1 head romaine lettuce
1 - 10 oz. can mandarin oranges
2 green onions, chopped finely
1/2 cup slivered almonds
1/4 cup white vinegar
1/4 cup granulated sugar
2 tbsp. orange liquid, reserved when draining oranges
1/4 cup salad oil

Tear lettuce into bite-sized pieces. Add drained oranges and green onions, and chill. Toast almonds at 350°F for 5 minutes. Mix salad oil, vinegar, and sugar with the orange liquid, shake well and chill. (These three steps can be done several hours ahead of your meal.) Just before serving, toss lettuce gently with dressing and sprinkle almonds on top.

Wondering what to serve your "after Christmas company" with your "after Christmas turkey"? You can't go wrong with this casserole.

Pineapple Almond Turkey Casserole

6 oz. broad noodles
2 tbsp. butter
1 tsp. salt
1 tbsp. flour
1 cup milk
1 can cream of chicken or mushroom soup
1-19 oz. can pineapple chunks, drained
2 tbsp. chopped green pepper (optional)
pinch of pepper
1 cup of blanched, slivered almonds
1 tsp. Worcestershire sauce
2 cups chopped, cooked turkey

Cook noodles as directed on package. Melt butter and saute green pepper. Remove green pepper, stir in flour, and add milk. Stir constantly until thickened. Stir in the rest of the ingredients and half of the almonds. Layer ingredients, begin with noodles and end with creamed mixture in a greased casserole. Sprinkle remaining almonds on top and bake at 350°F for 25 minutes.

Recipes for Children

If you are a mom, a teacher, a daycare supervisor or a Sunday school teacher, you'll love these recipes, and your children or students will remember them forever. What terrific memories you are making—and it's so easy!

☆ ☆ ☆

Reindeer Chow

1 handful of frosted shredded wheat squares (represents hay with snow from the North Pole)
1 handful of pretzel sticks (for tender twigs)
1 handful of raisins (for dried berries)
1 handful of red candies like M & M's (for fresh berries)
a baby carrot

Put all of the food items in a ziploc baggie. Close it up tight and shake well—kids love the shaking part! Add a note that says, "Even Santa's reindeer can use a snack now and then. Leave me out with cookies and milk for Santa and his reindeer on Christmas Eve." If you leave out the carrot (which would not stay fresh), kids can make up a few bags for a Christmas bazaar or craft sale. Change the note to say, "Add a baby carrot and leave me out for Santa and his reindeer."

☆ ☆ ☆

Bagel Wreaths

Cut mini-bagels in half. Give children softened cream cheese as well as some coconut that you've tinted green and let them decorate the bagels. Add some tiny pieces of chopped maraschino cherries for the berries! If you wish to make a healthier snack, use some fresh chopped parsley or lettuce and tiny bits of red pepper instead of coconut and cherries.

Reindeer Sandwiches

These are always a hit with youngsters. Why not make up a plateful with your own children and send another plateful to school? Or take the ingredients in and help the children make them for snack time. Cut brown bread into half diagonally and then cut again so you have four small triangles. Remove crusts if you wish. Spread with peanut butter. Put a piece of maraschino cherry on the bottom for the nose, two chocolate chips or raisins for the eyes, and two curved pretzels for the antlers. Make some to leave out for Santa!

Christmas Trees

These are great fun to make with the "under eight crowd."

Fasten an upside down ice cream cone to a paper plate with a dab of icing. Frost with green icing and decorate with candies, colored mini-marshmallows or fruit loops. Be sure to buy pointed cones.

Snowman Snack

Use two or three mini-rice cakes or popcorn cakes for the body. Spread with softened cream cheese to make white snow. Add raisins for the eyes, nose, mouth and buttons. A thin licorice whip or a carrot curl work well for the scarf.

CHAPTER 18

Kid-Tested Crafts

by Dylan
M.,
age 7

Children love to make crafts, and it's a terrific way to have fun together. When you spend time with your kids, you are letting them know that family time is important and that you enjoy their company. Your time and attention is a very special gift. The memories will last forever.

Choose two or three projects to try this year. Read the directions carefully from beginning to end, and make a list of all the craft supplies you'll need. Pick them up early in the fall when the selection in craft stores is at its best. Store all the materials together in a box or plastic tote bin with a lid. On craft night, cover your table with an inexpensive plastic tablecloth that can be reused. Remember to print the name of the child and the date on the back of each project. Keep some baby wipes on hand for quick clean ups, and have fun!

If you are making crafts with a large group of younger children, ask a couple of parents to precut some of the project pieces. They'll be glad to help. Make sure you provide a sample and very clear instructions of *exactly* what you would like your parent helpers to do.

Christmas Orange Wreath

Supplies:

7 or 8 Christmas oranges
10" by 24" inch piece of clear cellophane (or saran wrap)
three yards of one-inch wide Christmas ribbon (cut into 12" lengths)

Lay the oranges flat along the length of the cellophane rectangle. Leave a couple of inches between each orange, as well as on each end of the rectangle. Fold the cellophane over and turn the folded edge to the back. Fasten with tape. Tie Christmas ribbon where you've left spaces between the oranges. Gather the top edges of the cellophane together and fasten with a piece of twist tie. (Leave some of the cellophane on each end.) Tie a big ribbon bow on the top.

Wasn't that easy? These wreaths make a great gift for a teacher or daycare provider.

Santa Advent Calendar

Supplies:

a large, sturdy paper plate
skin-colored paint or crayon
red construction paper
white construction paper
crayons or felts
cotton puffs
glue

Color or paint the paper plate with a skin color for Santa's face. Draw the eyes, cheeks and mouth with crayons or felts. Glue cotton puffs on for the moustache. Paste a cherry nose on top of Santa's moustache. Add some cotton puff eyebrows and a red hat cut from construction paper. Make a beard shape from white paper and glue it on the bottom of the paper plate below the mouth. Print the numbers from 1 to 24 on the beard (or run off photocopied beards with the numbers on for a large group of kids). Decorate a paper lunch bag and put 24 cotton puffs inside. Each day children glue a puff on the appropriate number on Santa's beard. It makes more sense to kids if you put the first cotton puff on the number 24—the next day they know there are 23 days til Christmas, and so on. You'll know it's Christmas when Santa's beard is full!

Christmas Party Crackers

Supplies:

crepe paper or wrapping paper to cover tubes
leftover paper towel or wrapping paper tubes, cut into 5" lengths
ribbon or cord to tie ends of crackers
tiny gifts such as rings, earrings or toy cars from the dollar store
fortunes or jokes written on small slips of paper
snappers and paper hats are optional (available at craft stores)

Cut crepe paper or wrapping paper into 7" by 15" rectangles. If you have them, use pinking shears to cut the short edges. If you use plain colored crepe paper, run a line of white glue along both short edges and shake glitter over the glue for a really glamorous effect. Write a riddle, joke or fortune for each cracker and tuck it inside along with the gifts. Center your filled tube along the long edge of the wrapping paper. Fasten with plain tape. Roll the paper tightly around the tube and tape the seam shut. Gently tie a piece of ribbon or cord around each end.

Decorate with Christmas stickers or a name card for each guest. You can personalize the crackers for the guests who are coming or make them in two different colors—one for boys and men and another for girls and ladies. If you want to recycle the cracker covers next year, use fabric rather than paper to cover the tubes.

Gumdrop Wreaths

Supplies:

thin floral wire
a dull pair of scissors to cut the wire with
a package of red, white and green gumdrops
curling ribbon

Cut the wire into 12" lengths for small wreaths. Thread the gumdrops on. You may want to make a red, green and white pattern. Twist the top of the wire together. Tie on some ribbon and use dull scissors to make a curly ribbon bow. For a country look, the same technique can be used with cranberries. Twist the wire in a circle or heart shape and tie with a raffia bow.

Yummy Snowmen Table Favors

Supplies:

3 large marshmallows per snowman
fruit leather
straight pretzels
mini chocolate chips
large gumdrops and gumdrop rings
toothpicks

Push one long thin pretzel up through the middle marshmallow so part of it is showing on either end. Add another marshmallow on the top and the bottom. Wrap a piece of fruit leather around the neck for a scarf. Poke chocolate chips through the top marshmallow to make the eyes, mouth, and nose. Poke two or three more through the middle one for buttons. Add pretzel arms. Put a flat gumdrop ring on the top marshmallow to form the base of the hat, then add a regular gumdrop to form the top. Fasten the hat to the head with a toothpick. These snowmen make cute decorations for the Christmas table. Your children could also make some for their class at school. (Make sure toothpicks are taken out before eating.)

Fruit Loop Christmas Trees

Supplies:

Fruit Loops
green and yellow construction paper
white glue in a squeeze
bottle

Fold a 9" by 12" piece of green construction paper in half. Cut a triangle-shaped Christmas tree with a base, using pinking shears or regular scissors. Cut out a star shape from yellow paper for the children to glue on the top of the tree. Children put dots of glue where they would like their decorations to go, then drop Fruit Loops on top. If you are working with a large group of children, you'll probably want to precut the trees and stars. Preschool children can make these successfully.

Votive Candle Holder

Supplies:

red and green tissue paper, torn in small pieces
white glue
small baby food jars (soak well to remove labels)
tea light candles
kindergarten sized paintbrush

Pour the white glue into a recycled container and dilute it slightly with water. Use an old paintbrush to paint the glue mixture all over the outside of the baby food jar. When the children put the tissue pieces on top of the glue, they should press each piece down well around the edges. Cover the entire jar and let it dry well. Put the tea light candle inside and you have a great gift!

A delightful way to present the gift is to give it along with a card with a construction paper candle on the outside. Add some glitter to make it sparkle. Inside the card write, "Because you light up my life." Any grandma or grandpa would treasure this special gift.

Craft Stick Snowmen

Supplies:

jumbo craft sticks
scraps of black construction paper
white acrylic paint
small paintbrush
white glue in a squeeze bottle or low-melt glue gun and glue sticks
tiny twigs for arms (nice, but not absolutely necessary)
ribbon to make a loop hanger

If you have lots of time, collect small twigs a couple of days before beginning this project and let them dry well. (If not, they look cute without arms too.) Paint the whole jumbo craft stick white. Let the front dry, then flip it over and paint the back. It makes sense to make several snowmen at once; they look cute tied on parcels! Cut out hats from the black construction paper and glue one on top of each stick. Use felt pens to add black eyes and an orange nose. Tiny buttons or beads may be glued on the middle for buttons. A scarf can be made from scraps of fabric, felt, or construction paper. Glue on the tiny twigs for arms as well as a ribbon loop on the back to hang the ornament from.

Craft Stick Santas

Supplies:

jumbo craft sticks
regular popsicle-sized craft sticks, cut in half
red acrylic paint
small paintbrush
recycled margarine lid to put paint in
scraps of white, red, pink and black construction paper
cotton puffs (or bits of real fleece)
scissors
white glue in squeeze bottle or low-melt glue gun and glue-stick

Paint the front of the jumbo craft stick and two halves of the smaller popsicle stick red. Let dry, then paint the backs. The large craft stick will be Santa's body. Glue the smaller pieces on the back of the jumbo stick to form the arms—angle them down slightly. When dry, cut out a circle from pink paper for Santa's face. Glue it one-quarter of the way down the jumbo stick. Add a red construction paper hat and glue it above the face. Cut out a simple belt from black construction paper and glue it half way down the body. Make black paper mittens and paste them on the ends of the arms.

Glue on cotton puffs or a bit of fleece for a beard. Add eyes and nose with felt pens. Glue a loop of ribbon on the back for a hanger.

Egg Carton Sleighs

These make wonderful gifts for family and friends, a seniors' center or a homeless shelter. We make them each year as decorations for Meals on Wheels trays. You could also make them for your child's classmates at school or day-care. (Use *very* small candies if giving the sleighs to children.) Make lots—they look great when used as place cards on the table for a children's party or for Christmas dinner. They go together easily and kids and adults love them. When we make them for seniors, we use the plain red and green M & M's since some people have peanut allergies.

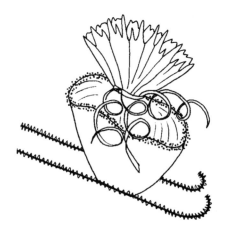

Supplies:

corrugated cardboard egg cartons
one red pipe cleaner per sleigh, cut in half
green tempera paint
a small paintbrush
white glue in a squeeze bottle or low-melt glue gun and glue sticks

glitter—multicolored or silver or gold
a recycled plastic lid to shake the glitter into
small candies
small squares of saran wrap
curly ribbon
a homemade or purchased gift tag for each sleigh

An adult needs to cut the egg carton apart into individual cups. Cut the front a little lower than the back to give the appearance of a sleigh. Paint the cups and let them dry. Painting one day and decorating the next works well. Shake some glitter in a margarine lid. Run a bead of glue around the top edge of the painted egg cup and then dip it in the glitter. Let dry.

Bend the front of the two pipe cleaner pieces to form curved runners and glue the egg carton sleigh on top of them. Use a good tacky craft glue or a low-melt glue gun. Let dry well.

Put six or seven small candies into each square of saran wrap, fold the top edges together, and tie with ribbon. Use dull scissors to curl the ribbon, then tuck the tiny bundles of candy into the seats of the sleighs. Tie gift tags to each bundle of candy with the recipient's name on if you know who you are giving the sleigh to or just write "Merry Christmas from ..."

Shell Santa Ornaments

If you have access to clam or oyster shells, these ornaments are a wonderful project. If you don't live near the ocean, ask someone who does to save you a few shells (or purchase them at a craft store). Primary-aged children can make these with some help. Older children won't need much assistance.

Supplies:

a clam or oyster shell for each necklace
an electric drill
red or burgundy, white, skin-colored and black acrylic paint
pink, red and blue felt pens
a small white pom-pom for each Santa (optional)
clear acrylic sealer spray
thin satin ribbon—red, burgundy, white or green
paintbrushes

If you found your shells on the beach, an adult should boil them to make sure they are really clean—add a few drops of bleach to make sure. Let the shells dry well, and then use an electric drill to make a small hole in the top of each one. Use the natural shape of the shell to 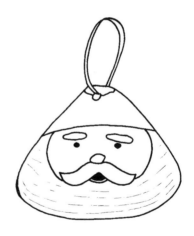 design Santa's face. Oyster shells work especially well because the wrinkles form wonderful beards. Use the natural contours to decide where to place the nose and eyes. Clam shells make a more modern Santa. Use the wider, round part for the bottom of the beard.

Draw a hat on the top part and sketch an oval shape just below it for the face. Paint the hat red or burgundy. Let it dry. Paint the face a skin color and let it dry. If necessary, touch up the white part of the shell for the beard, and paint a white moustache. Let it dry, then add a red nose, two blue eyes and two pink cheeks with felt pens. An adult may spray the ornaments with clear acrylic sealer in a well-ventilated area. Glue a white pom-pom on the top part of Santa's hat before threading the ribbon through the hole. Use a long ribbon if you are making a necklace and a shorter one for an ornament.

Christmas Garlands

If you don't know what to do with your packing peanuts (those styrofoam s-shapes), give them to your children to

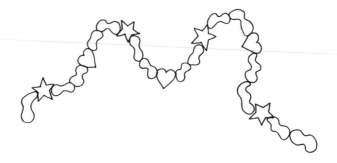

string. They don't crumble as easily as popcorn. If you want to make the garland more attractive, add a big button every few inches. You can purchase a bag of big buttons and a very large blunt needle at a craft store. Dental floss also makes a sturdy thread.

·☆· ·☆· ·☆·

Easy Gingerbread Houses

Kids love making their own tiny gingerbread houses. It's easy when you use graham crackers. To make the base more stable, save small half-pint milk cartons to use as a foundation for the house. Your walls won't collapse!

Supplies:

graham wafers
a sturdy paper plate as a base
a well-rinsed half-pint milk carton
plastic knives
royal icing (Buy the powdered mixture for the icing at your local craft or cake decorating supply store. It is safer than the homemade recipe made with raw egg whites.)
an assortment of candies

Cover each side of the milk carton with royal icing and one graham cracker. (Have younger children work with an older child in a buddy system.) Use two crackers, one on each side, to make a peaked roof on the top; the slope of the milk carton helps you make the roof easily. Let the house dry before gluing on the decorations with the royal icing.

Because these houses are not very big, small candies look more attractive. Fasten the house to the paper plate with more royal icing. Use some green gumdrops as trees around the base of the house.

If you are working with a large group of children, ask each child to bring a cup of candy because it can get quite expensive. Shake some of each type of candy into several containers so each group has an assortment to choose from. For a pioneer Christmas, children can turn their house into a rustic log cabin by covering the graham cracker foundation with straight pretzels placed lengthwise along the walls and by adding shreddies for shingles on the roof.

Pasta Wreaths

I've had great success making these wreaths with 3 to 6 year-olds. A little advance preparation really helps.

Supplies:

sturdy dinner-sized paper plates
yellow, red and green food coloring
assorted uncooked pasta—look for interesting shapes
a hole punch
wool or thin ribbon for the hanger
red construction paper for a big bow
white glue in squeeze bottles

You'll need to cut out a circle from the center of the paper plates ahead of time. Use a small saucer as a tracer. Collect different sorts of pasta; wheels and bows look great. It's easy to color the uncooked pasta; put 1 tsp. of food coloring, 2 tbsp. of rubbing alcohol, and 1 cup of dry pasta into a ziploc baggie and shake well. Let it dry on wax paper or on a cookie sheet. An adult should dye all the pasta ahead of time because the food coloring can stain clothing. Afterwards make sure the rubbing alcohol is put away in a safe place. Prepare red, yellow, and green pasta.

Cut out some simple red bows from construction paper. Have the children paint the front of the paper plates green; let them dry well before decorating. Decide where the bow will go first and glue it on. Have the children put a dab of white glue everywhere they want to put a decoration and drop pasta on the glue. Punch a hole in the top and thread wool or ribbon through to make a hanger.

Button Trees

Supplies:

white glue
small buttons
mediumweight cardboard (green or plain)
yellow construction paper

Cut simple tree shapes from cardboard. You can use a recycled cereal box and have the children paint the trees green, or you can purchase green posterboard. Children glue the buttons on with white glue. Glue a yellow paper star on the top of the tree and use the hole punch to make a hole at the top for the ribbon to go through.

A variation on this project is to cut out red cardboard candy canes and use small white buttons to make the stripes. If you want to make fridge magnets rather than tree ornaments, buy lightweight wooden shapes at your craft store, paint them, glue on the buttons and then fasten a piece (or two) of magnetic tape to the back of each one.

Snow Globes

Supplies:

recycled baby food jar
mineral oil (available at the drug store)
pearly white or silver glitter
tiny plastic miniatures (pick them up on sale after Christmas and put them away for next year)
strong craft glue

Wash the jar well. If you want a more attractive globe, paint the outside of the jar lid with acrylic paint, or have an adult spray the lids in a well-ventilated area. Put dabs of glue on the inside of the lid, and then drop the tiny miniatures onto the glue. Let dry for a few hours. Fill the jar with mineral oil and sparkles. Make sure a grownup screws the lid on really well. Older children enjoy making these. Younger ones enjoy shaking them!

Jigsaw Puzzle Wreaths

Supplies:

jigsaw puzzle pieces (from your local thrift store)
inexpensive gold or green spray paint
mediumweight cardboard such as a cereal box
large sequins or small pom-poms
wool or ribbon
pre-made bows from the ornament section of your craft store
heavy-duty craft glue

Cut out a dinner plate sized cardboard circle. Use a smaller plate to trace the inner circle of the wreath. Cut an X in the center circle and cut it out. (Ask a helper or two to prepare the wreaths ahead of time.) Children glue a layer of jigsaw pieces on the circle, putting the glue on the plain side of the jigsaw puzzle pieces. Add another layer on top of the first one, overlapping the pieces. Press down really firmly to make sure the pieces are secure. Let dry overnight.

An adult should spray paint the wreaths in a well ventilated area. Gold or green wreaths are both attractive. Wear an inexpensive paper face mask available at the hardware store when using spray paint. Let dry overnight. Give children sequins or pom-poms and a bow to glue on their wreath. To make the hanger, tape a paper clip on the back, and thread a piece of thin ribbon or wool through it. Children can make tiny wreaths to glue their photographs behind for inexpensive gifts.

So Simple Napkin Rings

Supplies:

an empty paper towel tube
Christmas ribbon or felt
small shapes cut from recycled Christmas cards or tiny artificial poinsettias
craft glue

An adult should cut the paper towel tube into widths that match the width of the Christmas ribbon. Strips of felt can be used instead of ribbon if you wish. Wrap the ribbon or felt strip around the tube and glue it down. Add some sequin trim or a narrower satin ribbon or lace. Glue a Christmas card cutout or small artificial flower 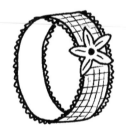 on the front. Your children will be very proud when their creations decorate the Christmas table. Classes at school or Brownies or Cubs can make some to decorate trays at a nearby hospital or seniors' home. Slide a plain red dinner napkin through each napkin ring and send them along with your best wishes for a happy holiday.

Scented Cinnamon Ornaments

Supplies:

1 cup of cinnamon (pick up at your bulk food store)
1 tsp. of cloves
1 tsp. of nutmeg
3/4 cup of applesauce
2 tsp. of white glue
puffy paints
tiny buttons

In a medium bowl, combine the spices. Add applesauce and glue and stir to combine. Work mixture well with hands for 2 to 3 minutes until the dough is very smooth and the ingredients are thoroughly mixed. Divide the dough into four portions. Roll each out to 1/4 inch thickness. Cut shapes from dough with cookie cutters. Hearts or gingerbread men both make attractive ornaments. Poke holes through the top of each ornament with short pieces of a straw. Leave the straw in place until ornaments are dry. Place cutouts on wire racks and dry at room temperature for several days. Turn ornaments over two or three times a day for more even drying. Decorate with puffy paints and tiny buttons. They look great on parcels wrapped in brown paper or tied onto a wreath. Remind children these delightful decorations are not to be eaten. Children can make a batch for your school's craft sale or your church's bazaar.

Mini Wreaths

Supplies:

small grapevine wreaths (5" or 6" in diameter)
fir or cedar greenery, cut in short lengths
tiny pine cones
ribbon or pre-made bows
thin ribbon for a hanger
craft glue

When choosing the wreaths, look for loosely woven ones with lots of open spaces so children can squeeze the pieces of fir or cedar in easily. You can find small wreaths at almost any craft or dollar store. Tuck in fan-shaped pieces of greenery. Glue or wire a few tiny pine cones on, add a bow and tie a thin piece of ribbon around the top for a hanger. These wreaths can also be used as a centerpiece with a fat candle inside. Be *very* careful when using candles in a centerpiece and never leave it unattended.

CHAPTER 19

Handmade With Love

By Nicole & Kristen   Age 10 + 9

I made a Santa necklace for my mom. She said she would wear it every Christmas. My mom likes homemade presents best.

by Sophie L, age 8

"The gift you give to another
Need not be an expensive thing
As long as you've tucked some love inside
Before you tie the string."
~ Anonymous

Children of all ages love making gifts for family and friends. When you make gifts together, you are helping your children develop their creativity. You are also enhancing their self-esteem by developing their sense of competence. But the most important reason for making gifts is to help your children understand that giving gifts is as important as receiving them. A gift can say "I love you, I appreciate you, and I care about you." A handmade gift says all of this more eloquently—these treasures made by tiny hands leave a special impression on the hearts of the lucky recipients.

Early in November, help your children make a list of friends and relatives they would like to make presents for. Set aside some time each week for the next month to work on handmade gifts. Try to be finished by the end of the first week in December. You want your craft time to be enjoyable, not another "have to do" item on your long list.

All of these projects have been tested with children from two to fifteen with great results.

Hands and Feet Reindeer

You can make a simple muslin banner or decorate a T-shirt or sweatshirt with your children's footprints. These very special reindeer are sure to be a big hit with grandparents.

Supplies:

a T-shirt or sweat shirt or a muslin banner (banner requires a thin wooden dowel)
brown, red, and black acrylic paint
fabric medium to add to the acrylic paint if making a washable shirt (follow the instructions for mixing found on the bottle)
recycled plastic container lids to pour the paint in
a large craft paintbrush
a jingle bell, needle and thread
1/2 yard of narrow red or green satin ribbon or wool

If you are making a banner, cut a muslin rectangle, fold over the top edge and sew a straight seam to form a casing to insert a thin dowel into. Cut the bottom edges to a point. You don't need to finish the edges of the banner; use pinking shears or leave them unfinished.

Assemble all the items you need along with an ice cream pail with warm water, a bar of soap, and an old towel. Paint the sole of your child's foot with brown paint and stamp it on the muslin or T-shirt. It's important *not* to paint the toes or your reindeer will look funny! Wash and dry off foot. Paint both hands with black paint and carefully position them to form the two antlers. Wash and dry hands. Dab thumb in red paint to form the nose, then wash thumb. Dab pointer finger in black paint and dab on eyes. Wash pointer. After the banner or T-shirt has dried, you can add, or have your child add,

"Noel," "Joy," or "For a Dear Grandma." You may be able to fit two smaller children's footprints on one banner or T-shirt. If you are making a banner, sew a jingle bell on the bottom and tie the ribbon on both ends of the dowel.

If you think this project is too messy, just trace your children's hands on black paper and their foot on brown paper, then combine to make a paper reindeer. These can be tucked in a Christmas scrapbook and are fun to look at each year. Your children will enjoy seeing how much their hands and feet have grown. You can also paste them on a hand-made card to delight a special relative.

Handprint Wreath

I have made these with children on muslin banners as well as on good quality paper.

Supplies:

red and green acrylic paint (you can use tempera with paper)
a muslin banner (about 14" by 14")
a thin dowel
red or green 1/4 inch satin
ribbon

Cut out the muslin and use pinking shears if you have them to finish the side and bottom edges. Fold the top edge over an inch and a half and sew a casing. Trace a small circle with a saucer

in the center of the banner as a guide to show where to place the handprints. Put green paint on an ice cream pail lid. Press your child's hand in the green paint and go around the circle building a wreath. Turn hand toward the inside of the circle sometimes to fill in the center of the wreath. Wash hands, then dip a finger in red paint and dab on several berries. You can paint a red bow on with a finger or make a bow from ribbon and tack it on. Be sure to put your child's name and the date on with a permanent fine-tipped felt pen.

Grandparents LOVE these special banners. Print the following poem on a plain file card, (adjusting the name to suit the person you are giving it to) and fasten it with a small safety pin to the banner:

> *My little handprints made this wreath,*
> *My tiny thumbs each berry,*
> *And Grandma, I hope this helps you have*
> *A Christmas that's extra merry.*
> *I love you Grandma!*

Popsicle Stick Picture Frames

Supplies:

8 wooden popsicle sticks for each frame (you can buy packages which are already stained various colors or paint your own)
acrylic paint
thin wooden hearts, trees, snowmen (or stars or sequins or metallic confetti)
craft glue or low-melt glue gun and glue stick
a photograph of your child
a strip of magnetic tape or ribbon
paintbrushes

Help your child paint the popsicle sticks. Choose a color that compliments the photograph you have chosen. If you are decorating the frame with wooden shapes, paint them at the same time. Allow the sticks to dry, then glue them together to form the frame.

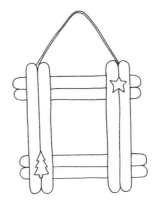

Lay down the popsicle sticks in pairs to form a square. Glue the left and right hand sets on top of the top and bottom pairs, moving the ends in slightly. Glue on some sequins, confetti trees or snowflakes or the wooden shapes you've already painted to dress up the frames. Glue your child's picture on the back and add a strip of magnetic tape on the top and the bottom or tie on some ribbon so it can hang on the tree.

I Love You Mugs

Supplies:

an inexpensive ceramic mug from the dollar store
special craft paints designed for ceramics
paintbrushes

Wash and dry the mugs well first with warm water and vinegar. Have your child plan what he/she wants to draw first on a piece of paper—you can't go wrong with white snowmen on a blue mug. Follow the manufacturer's instructions for the paints and have fun. Remember to add your child's name and the date on the bottom. Put some hot chocolate packages inside the mug and tie up with cellophane and curly ribbon. Although many of the paint products available will make a dishwasher-safe mug, they'll last longer if washed by hand.

Christmas Candles

It's fun to make beeswax candles with children. They are quite easy to do if you warm the wax gently with a blow dryer as you roll them up. Simple shapes are best for small children. To build short, chubby candles, just cut each sheet lengthwise into four rectangles, lay the wick down, allowing an inch to hang over one end, and roll the wax up slowly. An adult needs to help by keeping it rolled tightly. You can cut decorations from a contrasting color of wax with tiny cookie cutters. Holly and berries are attractive on a natural colored candle. Press the decorations on carefully after warming up the area where you are attaching them. Candles make a nice gift when given with a card that says:

I made this candle by myself,
It comes wrapped up with my love.
Thanks for being my special ————-.
Love ——————-.

☆   ☆   ☆

If you are looking for a simple gift to give to a family or your favorite hostess, try this cookie mix-in-a-jar recipe. You can make several batches at once. Busy moms and kids alike will love the smell of fresh baking without all the fuss of mixing and measuring.

Cookie Mix-in-a-Jar

Children love these colorful cookie mixes—they make great fundraisers for a bake sale as well. (Use the plain M & M's since some children have peanut allergies.) You'll need:

a one-quart wide mouth Mason jar, lid and screw top
1 cup brown sugar
1/2 cup white sugar
1 cup plain M & M's (packages of red and green ones are sold near Christmas)
2 cups flour
1 tsp. salt
1 tsp. baking powder

Mix the salt and baking soda with the flour in a bowl. Layer half of the flour, salt, and soda mix, then half of the white sugar, half of the brown, and ALL of the M & M's at one time in the jar. (Pat down the brown sugar layers VERY firmly.) Now layer the other half of the brown sugar, white sugar, flour, salt and soda mix. (You may have to tap the jar gently on the counter to get all of the top layer of flour in.)

Use pinking shears to cut a 9-inch circle of Christmas fabric to cover the lid. Place the fabric circle over top of the sealed jar and secure it with a rubber band. Cover the rubber band with a raffia or ribbon bow. Attach a card with the following mixing and baking instructions.

Cookie Mix-in-a-Jar

Preheat oven to 350°F. Cream 1 cup of butter or margarine. Add 1 egg and 1 tsp. vanilla. Add cookie mix-in-a jar. Mix until well-blended. Drop by teaspoonfuls onto greased baking sheet. Bake 8 to 10 minutes.

·☆· ·☆· ·☆·

Children can also help mix up this delicious brownie recipe for an inexpensive gift.

Brownie Mix-in-a-Jar

a one-quart wide mouth Mason jar, lid and screw top
2 1/4 cups white sugar
2/3 cup cocoa
1/2 cup chopped walnuts or pecans
1 1/4 cup flour
1 tsp. baking powder
1 tsp. salt
1/4 cup of white or chocolate chips (optional)

Mix the baking powder, salt and flour together and set aside. Layer the other ingredients in a one-quart wide mouth canning jar. Wipe the inside of the jar with a dry paper towel after adding the cocoa powder. Press each layer down very firmly before adding the flour mixture last.

If layering the ingredients seems too fiddly, just mix the dry ingredients together in a ziploc bag and put the bag inside a festive fabric bag you've sewn. Attach the following directions to the jar or bag.

Brownie Mix-in-a-Jar

Empty the brownie mix into a large mixing bowl. Stir well with a fork. Add 3/4 cup of melted butter and 4 slightly beaten eggs. Mix until well blended. Spread batter into a greased 9" x 13" baking pan. Bake at 350°F for 30 minutes. Cool completely in the pan. Ice if you wish or just add some chocolate chips to the batter. Cut into 2-inch squares.

I'm sending you these tiny gifts and know you'll understand
Why I'd rather send you something that I made myself by hand.
~ A Victorian Christmas Card

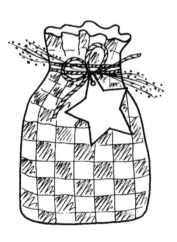

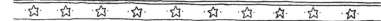

CHAPTER 20

Wrapping It All Up

Mom

Dad

Me

Matraca P., 8

I made these for you.

> *"Fond are the memories I have of opening Christmas cards*
> *and thinking myself loved."*
> *~ Anonymous*

Handmade cards, tags and wrap are simple for children to create and make gifts more personal. Use some of your children's drawings as Christmas cards this year—color copiers make it easy to do. Your local office supply store will be glad to help. Use your duplicate family photos as gift tags and add glitter glue, stars or stickers. You can also design your own gift wrap using photos; paste them on a sheet of 11" by 17" photocopy paper and visit an office supply store to have copies made. Black and white photos look great and are much less expensive to copy. Grandparents and other relatives will love gifts wrapped with your family's unique tags and paper.

Brown Bag It

It's amazing what you can do with a brown lunch bag. Children can add drawings or glitter glue designs or turn the bag into a house by adding construction paper doors and windows. Add touches like tiny paper trees and a wreath on the door. Put the gift inside before stapling a folded piece of construction paper on top to make the roof. A snowman and snow scene are also attractive. Cut a snowman, snow bank and trees from construction paper. Add details with paper and crayons.

Teens or adults can use fusible interfacing to make easy appliques from Christmas fabric to iron onto brown bags. Look for fabric that has a design with small squares or rectangles printed on it. Follow the directions on the fusible interfacing. Iron the whole piece of fabric onto a piece of fusible interfacing which you have cut the same size as your fabric. Cut around each square or rectangle, and fuse them individually onto the paper bag. If the design is quite small, you'll want to put several appliques on each bag. Fold the top of the bag over and hole punch two holes. Insert a piece of ribbon or raffia through the holes.

Use your gingerbread man cookie cutter to make tree ornaments or tags from brown paper bags too. Decorate them with puffy fabric paints and glue on tiny buttons or ric-rack.

Pom-Pom Tags

Supplies:

1 inch red, white and green pom-poms
1/4 inch pom-poms (the sparkly kind look great)
white, green or red lightweight cardboard
tacky craft glue
a hole punch
thin satin ribbon or wool
a yard or so of half-inch wide plaid ribbon, depending on how many tags you are going to make

Precut rectangles and squares from the cardboard. Try turning a cardboard square diagonally so it looks like a diamond. Form a wreath with green pom-poms. Glue them in a circle. Add some tiny red pom-poms for berries. Make a plaid bow to glue on the bottom of the wreath. Write the recipient's name in the center of the wreath with a red felt pen. Punch a hole in the top of the tag and thread thin ribbon or wool through. You can also spell out the recipient's name or build a tree or snowman with pom-poms!

Holiday Cards

Supplies:

good quality 8 1/2" by 11" white paper
red and green liquid tempera or acrylic paint
glitter pens, glitter glue, or white glue and loose glitter
stencilling paintbrush

Experiment on some scrap paper first before using good quality paper. Fold the paper in half, short side to short side, and then fold the other way to make a card. Put some green paint onto the brush, then dab it several times on a scrap of paper to get rid of the excess paint. Pounce up and down, much like painting stencils, to create your basic shape. For a wreath, create a circle. For a tree, paint three overlapping triangles. Experiment with painting a border all the way around the card. Let the card dry before adding your decorations. With glitter glue or white glue and loose glitter, create berries, bows and ornaments. For a sparkly, snowy look, dab a little white paint on your trees and frost the tips of the white branches with white glue before sprinkling crystal or white glitter on top.

Angel Cards

Supplies:

9" by 12" sheet of blue construction paper
two medium-sized round white paper doilies
scraps of pink construction paper for hands and face
wool scraps or felt for hair
cotton balls for clouds
white glue
gold or silver glitter glue (or white glue and loose glitter)

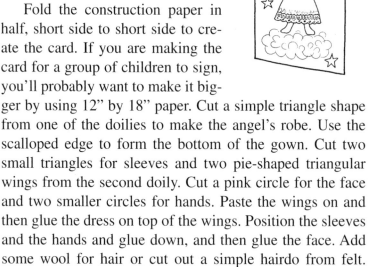

Fold the construction paper in half, short side to short side to create the card. If you are making the card for a group of children to sign, you'll probably want to make it bigger by using 12" by 18" paper. Cut a simple triangle shape from one of the doilies to make the angel's robe. Use the scalloped edge to form the bottom of the gown. Cut two small triangles for sleeves and two pie-shaped triangular wings from the second doily. Cut a pink circle for the face and two smaller circles for hands. Paste the wings on and then glue the dress on top of the wings. Position the sleeves and the hands and glue down, and then glue the face. Add some wool for hair or cut out a simple hairdo from felt. (Children like to match the angel's hair to their own hair color.) Add the eyes, nose and mouth with felt pens. Stretch out a cotton ball to make a cloud and glue it below the angel's feet. Add a gold or silver halo and make several stars in the sky; glitter glue or a gold pen makes it easy to do! You can also use regular white glue and then shake some loose glitter over top of the glue.

Inside the card, write:

*"My grandma (or mom or auntie or teacher) is an angel.
Thanks for all you do. Merry Christmas, love..."*

We've also used these angels to make thank you cards for our parent helpers or pasted several on a mural to thank businesses in our community for donations to school events.

My grandma has cancer. I hope we can find a cure soon. Thank you for buying this book.

Kaitlyn G.
age 9

I love you
Grandma

Love
Kaitlyn

Index

Gifts From The Heart makes a wonderful gift for family and friends!

Order extra copies from your favorite bookstore or directly from the publisher.

Make cheque or money order payable to "We Believe Publications." Prices are subject to change after Jan. 1st each year. Please allow three to four weeks for delivery. If faster delivery than parcel post is required, we will send orders by courier at your request and expense. Please contact us by email: vlbrucker@telus.net for more information about shipping by courier or for volume sales and terms.

Thank you for your support!

Caitlin J.

WE BELIEVE PUBLICATIONS
P.O. Box 47, Nanoose Bay, BC, V9P 9J9
Phone and FAX: 250-468-9888

Please PRINT:

Name_____

Street_____

City_____

Province_____ Postal Code_____

If you would like your book(s) inscribed and autographed by the author, please PRINT the name(s) you would like included here:

_____

_____

Please send _____ copies of *Gifts From The Heart* at $16.95 each (Canadian funds) plus $4.00 per book for postage and handling. Total amount enclosed: $_____.